Contents

Preface

Andrew began reading at 14 months. His mother said he was reading fluently by the age of 3. By the time he entered school at 5, Andrew was showing quite unusual ability, not only in the area of language (he had gone some way to learning a number of foreign languages through reading 'phrase' books) but also in music and mathematics. A tape-recording of him reading one of his stories to the village school teacher reveals a richness of imagination and wit that would be quite extraordinary in any child. In a child of 5 it is almost alarming. Two years later the child can be heard explaining how he transcribed music from tunes he had heard on television, by working out the 'key signatures', the rhythms and the correct notation. He then moves on to problem-solving using a slide rule: 'Set X to D, 3, 5, C line to X. Under the 25 on C read the answer 875 on D. Rough check 4 times the product times 2 equals 8. So answer is 8.75.'

Andrew was undoubtedly a brilliant child. No-one believed that meeting the teaching and social needs of such a child would be easy. Children as extraordinary as Andrew are, by definition, very rare. Many of us may not meet his like in our lifetime. If we do, we are likely to recognise the very real and special needs they will have, and we are also likely to want to help them. What we are perhaps less ready to acknowledge is that among our children in school there will be many other children with exceptional abilities such as Fiona, Martin and Joanna whom we meet in this book. There are far more than we realise. Some will have been welcomed and encouraged to develop their talents to the full. Others may have been recognised, but their exceptional intelligence may have isolated them. And yet others, far too many others, will have found ways of deliberately or subconsciously suppressing or diverting their natural abilities because of social pressures to conform.

It cannot be right to accept situations where children find it necessary to dampen down their intellectual energy, or where they are discouraged from declaring their consequent frustration. Our role as parents and teachers must be to create appropriate and helpful environments for children, climates in which positive attitudes to themselves and to others can be developed and in which excitement and enthusiasm for learning can be shared.

Public interest in the education of exceptionally able children has tended to wax and wane according to current political and economic concerns. Whether or not such interest is topical or fashionable, the fact remains that exceptionally able children exist. They live within their families; they attend our schools; they are loved and cared for by their parents; and they are taught and guided by their teachers. Parents and teachers are not primarily concerned as to whether there is a national interest in certain labelled groups of children. They are concerned with individuals, with the child they know, and for whom they strive to do their best to promote a healthy and happy development. Exceptionally able children are first and foremost *children* and should be seen as such. Their need for love, understanding and acceptance is as great as it is for any other child. Love may be readily available to them. Understanding and acceptance may prove more difficult.

This book is about the growth of relationships and about children's educational needs with particular regard to exceptional development. It offers a perspective on children with exceptional abilities and discusses how, through greater awareness and better understanding, we might all contribute to improving their learning environments.

The first edition of the book was published in 1985 and it was revised and reprinted in 1998. Much of the text in the first and second editions is still relevant today and has been incorporated into this current revision. However, there have been significant and wide-ranging changes in all aspects of education during the last 20 years. We have also seen in schools a renewed interest in the education of able children, strongly supported by the government and the Department for Education and Skills (DfES). It has therefore been necessary to reflect these changes and developments in this third edition. Each chapter in the book has been substantially rewritten and new sections have been included.

Part 1 is now concerned with understandings and attitudes associated with exceptional ability. It looks at the social and emotional needs of highly able children from birth through to adolescence and considers how precocious or unusual development can affect the children's relationships and their attitude to work. Part 2 is concerned with educational provision and with developing partnerships between school and home to support the children's development. It covers school policy and organisation, curriculum provision, pastoral care and support, extra-curricular activities, partnership with parents and making best use of community links.

The picture presented by this book is a personal one, developed as a result of many years working with pupils, parents and teachers, and listening to children describe their experiences. The interpretation owes much to the author's own search for understanding about the growth of self-knowledge and the management of relationships. The approach is based on a belief that the many problems that face young people, their families and their schools require insights rather than prescription. A problem recognised and shared is halfway to a problem solved.

All children featured are based on case studies of children I have met and with whom I have worked, though the names and some details have been changed in the interests of maintaining confidentiality.

The book could not have been written without encouragement and support from many people with whom I have worked. Numerous colleagues and friends have contributed to my understanding about children and their needs. I am indebted to them all and I refer to the work of many of them in the course of the book. I am grateful to Marvin Close for his witty cartoons which bring a life and a lightness to the text and prevent it from being altogether too serious, to Ruth Larbey for her poem and to Gwen Goodhew for examples of teacher planning. I would like to thank Mary Fitzpatrick for her invaluable advice during the revision of the book and to Joan Freeman for permission to use quotations from her study of gifted children: *Gifted Children Grown Up*. My three sons taught me about the challenges and the joys of being a parent. Together we faced many of the issues that are explored in the course of the book, and I salute them for their courage and stamina in coming through the growing up process so well. I am deeply grateful to Gervase Leyden for his support and patience during the writing process and for the wisdom of his comments . Above all, my most sincere thanks are due to all the children and their parents whose experiences have provided the starting point for this book.

Susan Leyden
Gibsmere, Nottinghamshire
2002

PART 1

Exceptional Ability and its Implications

CHAPTER 1

Introduction: beyond normal expectations

Katie

Katie was a startlingly pretty child with a mass of auburn curls, huge blue eyes and dimples. She sang with a true, clear voice, took dancing and guitar lessons and enjoyed writing stories. She was an avid reader. She was also an outgoing child, very much at ease in the company of adults whom she liked to entertain with bright social conversation. She was confident in manner, even a little gracious. Her parents adored her; I disliked her on sight. For Katie was only three years old. Poor Katie. Apart from her doting parents, no-one felt comfortable in her presence. Everything about her jarred one's assumptions about children of her age.

First there was the contrast within the family. Both parents were in their late forties when Katie was born, and were usually mistaken as her grandparents. Then there was the mismatch between her age and the manner and content of her conversation. The unexpectedness of it, the discomfort of being addressed in such adult terms by such a tiny child, aroused a sense of indignation and disapproval in those who met her. On top of all this were the surprising accomplishments. A three-year-old is just not expected to be able to do all the things that she did, and with such evident enthusiasm. Katie was something special. She was an exceptional child – and no-one liked her.

Anthony

Anthony was another unusual child. A friend came to visit with Anthony, his nine-year-old son. We talked of this and that, of mundane affairs, ordinary concerns, until someone asked the boy about his interest in some science project. From an awkward and rather taciturn lad, he became transformed: his eyes lit up, his hands moved rapidly in the air, words poured forth, experiments explained in lengthy and (for us) confusing detail, theories proposed and references made that were beyond the understanding of any of those present. We listened with a feeling of amazement. I remember thinking that we were hearing something remarkable, that Anthony was displaying a level of understanding and knowledge that was not at all in keeping with his age. I was also aware of the general discomfort and unease that this was causing. We simply did not know how to respond. We understood almost nothing of what he was saying. He, on the other hand, was so engrossed in his subject, and so caught up in the telling, that he left no room at all for us to respond – even had we been able to follow his thinking. We were left to smile politely while uttering such meaningless comments as, 'How interesting. Is that so...? How fascinating'. Anthony's father later explained that the child was deeply unhappy and frustrated in school. He had been unable to make any friends, generally found most of the work far too easy and boring, and he was becoming daily more reluctant to attend school.

Fiona

Fiona was 16. She had joined a group of 'scholarship' students preparing for the Oxford and Cambridge examinations through a series of fortnightly seminars led by university lecturers. Fiona had achieved 'A*' grades in no fewer than 10 GCSE examinations. She subsequently gained five grade 'A's in her A-levels. She played the cello for a county orchestra, had a lovely singing voice and was a talented sportswoman into the bargain. During the seminar discussions it had become obvious to the other students that this girl's depth and breadth of knowledge was of a different order altogether from their own. She was clearly exceptional, even among the very ablest students. 'But,' said one member of the group, 'the really surprising thing about Fiona is that she is so nice!'

During my time working as an educational psychologist on a project for developing the curriculum for very able pupils, I had the opportunity to talk at length to dozens of children who had unusual talents and abilities, and to their parents. These three examples, and the stories told to me by the many other children I have met, epitomise the fundamental dilemmas presented by unusual development, dilemmas which need to be understood if they are ever to be resolved. They demonstrate in the simplest terms that the whole question of giftedness is one not so much of definition, identification, categorisation and provision, but of *relationships*. It is concerned with the responses of persons one to another, the communication and expression of feelings and the inclusion or exclusion of individuals and groups. It also has to do with the willingness of schools and families to work together to find ways of meeting children's educational and social needs. The main cause of the confusion, and sometimes ill-judged position-taking, regarding children of exceptional ability has been the failure to recognise that at the heart of the matter we are dealing not so much with a special endowment *inside* a person, but with what happens *between* people.

How do we make sense of this? The explanation can perhaps best be given by looking again at the encounters with the three young people described. What was significant about Katie's and Anthony's behaviour was not their behaviour as such but the reactions this provoked in those around them. The fact that little Katie, by the age of three, had developed language more consistent with that of a nine-year-old, and a social poise that appeared quite out of keeping with her age, was not a problem in itself. We are all aware that children grow, develop and acquire their living skills at greatly varying rates. Children are not expected to be at similar stages in their development at particular ages. We do, however, construct certain 'limits of expectation', our own mental yardsticks by which we measure each new encounter. We develop an understanding of that which we judge to be a reasonable, expected, 'normal' range of behaviours. These personal yardsticks are arrived at through both our personal and our shared experiences.

Yardsticks of 'normality' will of course be relative to the time, the place and the experience of those who share them. What is felt to be normal in one situation may not be so in another. Take, for example, the question of height. A person may be judged to be extremely tall in one setting yet quite normal in another. A pygmy may be a giant among his own tribe, yet taken for a midget in a group of Masai warriors. There are no absolutes in the questions of tallness or shortness. Extremes can only be judged in relation to the environment in which they occur. This will be true of any experience. A problem only arises where the occurrence of an experience, be it physical, social, emotional or intellectual, falls outside the normal expectations of those involved. As with Katie, the problem of the precocity of her language and social poise lay not in the child, but in the response it evoked from others, and consequently and most essentially, in the messages that passed from others to her, messages of surprise, wariness and disapproval.

The case of Anthony, the nine-year-old scientist, was similar, but with additional significant elements. His conversation, too, was startling to those around because of the incongruity between his age and the level of intellectual understanding and experience he displayed. But here the mismatch was dramatically compounded. With Katie, although her language and manner jarred and evoked unkind and unhelpful responses, at least it was possible to have a conversation with her, to share her interests and understand her enthusiasms. But Anthony was caught up in a world of thinking and pursuits beyond the understanding of those around him. We were left on the sidelines of his thinking, reduced to behaving as spectators, nodding politely at appropriate moments. Again, the problem could not be said to be Anthony's exceptional intelligence in itself. Given a different setting, given a different audience there would have been no problem. The problem lay in the mismatch between his understanding and that of the people around the table. We felt inadequate, but more importantly, Anthony himself probably felt alien, and no doubt frustrated by the fact that we clearly did not understand what he was talking about. He had not learned to take account of the people he was with and adjust his conversation to the social situation.

Fiona clearly demonstrates that exceptional ability *per se* is not necessarily a problem. No-one denied that her talents were many and varied, that in the pursuit of her many and varied interests she achieved levels to which few of us can aspire. She was indeed a 'gifted' young person. Yet the surprise for Fiona's companions was that *despite* her exceptional talents she was a pleasant person to have around. Her peers not only admired, and perhaps even envied, her; they also liked her. How had this come about? Why should her companions be surprised by her niceness? Why should they have expected her to be otherwise? Why should we expect someone who has highly developed skills and talents to be socially inept or unpopular? What kind of unhelpful stereotyping has grown up around the concept of exceptional ability and talent, and what damage could this do to children's personal development? It is not always the case. It seems that in other countries, in the USA for example, the assumptions that surround highly able individuals are very different from those held in Britain, and are altogether more positive.

This would seem to be the heart of the matter, and the focus of concern for children and parents alike. The real question is not, 'Is this a gifted or exceptional child?' or 'Do this child's abilities qualify her to belong to a particular category which I can accept is gifted?' It is rather, 'How can I understand what is going on between this child and me, between this child and others, and between this child and her world?' And therefore, 'How can I, as the more experienced adult, enhance and guide this young person's life in order that he or she may make the very best of all his or her talents and qualities, whatever these may be?'

In order to understand how we can support young people who show exceptional ability or talent we need to consider what it can be like to grow up feeling 'different' and how this might affect children's self-esteem, self-confidence and their desire to demonstrate their abilities. Once we have some insight into the dynamics of exceptional development we are in a better position to consider how we can provide a suitable learning and social environment in which their talents can flourish. But first we need to decide what we mean by exceptional ability.

CHAPTER 2

Exceptional development: definition and meanings

Understanding exceptional ability

It has always been difficult to agree on what we understand by 'ability', and in particular what we mean when we say a child has 'exceptional' ability or talent. For many years the understanding of 'intelligence' was linked to the concept of an 'intelligence quotient' or IQ, as measured by specifically designed tests. Some of these are based on concepts of ability that date from the work of Binet who devised the first intelligence test. The Wechsler Intelligence Scale (WISC) and the British Ability Scales (BAS) are still used today. On these standardised tests a person's performance can be measured and compared with others of a similar age. A scale can be drawn up, with cut-off points at which the person's performance can be said to fall within, below or above the normal range. Exceptional ability would therefore be defined as performance that fell at the top of the scale, which only a small percentage of the population would achieve.

But human abilities cover a much wider spectrum than can be explored by such tests. The current view is to think of intelligence as multi-faceted, made up of factors that may be relatively independent of each other. There is also a far greater appreciation that social and cultural factors may determine how a person performs and influence what is valued.

One of the most influential models proposed in recent years is that of Howard Gardner, professor of Neurology at Boston University School of Medicine and also professor at the Harvard Graduate School of Education. He concluded that we have seven (and more recently, eight) intelligences:

- Linguistic (the ability to use language)
- Logical and Mathematical (the ability to reason, calculate and think logically)
- Visual-spatial (the ability to paint, draw and sculpt)
- Musical (the ability to compose, play an instrument and sing)
- Bodily-kinesthetic (physical and manipulative skills)

- Inter-personal (the ability to relate well to others)
- Intra-personal (self-awareness, the ability to know oneself)
- Naturalistic (awareness of the natural world and the ability to collect, categorise and analyse).

(Gardner 1983, 1990)

According to Gardner, our ability to understand and make sense of the world requires the use of all eight intelligences. A person can demonstrate unusual levels of ability in *all* areas of their development, or in any one sphere. Gardner suggests that very able people are more likely to show particular ability in one or in a combination of abilities than in all of them. He also proposed that each form of intelligence generates its own form of creativity. Very creative individuals have the ability to change the domain in which they manifest their particular talents. Exceptional ability would therefore be defined as unusually high-level or high-quality performance in terms of the particular areas of intelligence.

Other psychologists have put forward different models of intelligence. Sternberg's Triarchic Theory of Intelligence divides ability into analytical, creative and practical intelligences. These form the components of what Sternberg calls 'successsful' intelligence. This enables a person to recognise and demonstrate their individual strengths while finding ways of compensating and making adjustments for any limitation and weakness. Sternberg considers the ability to plan, monitor and evaluate their own thinking to be one of the key factors that distinguishes the skills of more able pupils (Sternberg 1985). This approach to thinking about intelligence is gaining in importance as increasing account is taken of different community and cultural priorities.

Another way of thinking about exceptional ability is to see it in terms of 'precocious' development where a child understands things or demonstrates behaviour at a much earlier age than might be expected. John Stuart Mill would be an example of a precocious child.

John Stuart Mill

John studied Greek at the age of 3; by the time he was 4 he was reading classical work fluently, he was studying physics and chemistry at a theoretical level before he was 11 and had written two essays on political economy by the age of 16. Galton, in the early nineteenth century, was also competent in Latin by the age of 4 and had read the *Iliad* and the *Odyssey* by the age of 6. He then turned his attention to physics and chemistry, and by 13 had designed a flying machine.

Alternatively, the behaviour of children with exceptional abilities may not be characterised only by its precocity, but also by the nature of their accomplishments and the quality of their performance. They may do things in unusual ways, look for interesting and novel solutions, find links between ideas and activities that others have not considered, or deliberately choose complex ways of doing things. Their ability to use language in creative and surprising ways may bring a distinctive quality to their writing. Their approach to work and play may be noticeable by its intensity, its heightened sense of purpose and its pursuit of perfection. William Hamilton is one example.

William Hamilton

William was reading Latin, Greek and Hebrew by the age of 5 and could recite long passages of Homer and Milton; he added a new language each year and by the age of 13 had a competent grasp of 13 languages, including Sanskrit and Persian. Pablo Picasso's extraordinary artistic skills were evident from a very early age and by the age of 14 he could paint as well as the Great Masters.

It is clearly easier to recognise high ability in whatever form it might manifest itself if children show this precocious development, or this high-level, intense or unusual response, through their approach to their work. Recognising the abilities of such children is not a problem.

Few of us, however, will encounter such people, or be charged with the responsibility for their education and upbringing. But many of us will be involved in one way or another with children who have the potential for exceptional attainment, in the field of academic study, sport or the creative arts. We are also likely to be involved with children who are unable or unwilling to show their potential talents, who do not perform well on the tests we give them, who have lost interest in their work or have chosen to mask their abilities in order to keep in with the crowd. Einstein was by all accounts an indifferent student during his school years, as were many other people who later made outstanding contributions in their own field of work.

Definitions

In Britain the term 'gifted' was widely used until well into the 1980s to describe children whose performance on standardised tests of intelligence placed them in the top 5 or 10 per cent of their age group. But there were continual arguments and debate as to what this really meant. Many people were uneasy with the term, feeling that it in some way disparaged other children not so defined. 'All my pupils are "gifted",' teachers would say. 'They all have gifts to offer, so why should only exceptional ability be singled out?' There was also disquiet about the possibility of the term clumping all 'highly able' children together and thinking about them as a single homogeneous group when, in reality, abilities, talents, personalities, learning styles and needs are so diverse.

Concepts of ability have changed and, as a result, the term 'gifted' faded away to be replaced by other descriptors. For some time the DfEE and OfSTED used 'Higher Attaining Pupils' in their reports and documents. This was not entirely satisfactory as it failed to take account of pupils with the potential for achieving at a very high level but who were performing below their capabilities. More recently, the government's Excellence in Cities (DfEE 1999) initiative has reintroduced the term gifted. 'Gifted and Talented' is now the required terminology in Britain for talking about pupils themselves and for provision that is made for them in schools.

There are, in fact, over 100 ways of describing ability that is 'above the norm'. Able, more able, very able, the most able, highly able, to name but a few. The term chosen for this book is 'children with exceptional ability'. Though this may seem a more cumbersome approach, it makes the distinction between the children's behaviour or performance and the children themselves as individuals. Everyone is unique, and in that respect everyone is exceptional. Children with exceptional abilities or talents are children first and foremost and their needs will be much the same as those of any other children. However, the rate of their development and the way they perform, or could perform, are unusual for their age group or the community in which they live and work.

Exceptional ability in the context of this book is therefore taken to be a level of ability in a particular sphere of activity that is unusual in terms of its quality or level of performance for the population in which it occurs.

CHAPTER 3

Infancy and the preschool years

Infancy

The origins of relationships

Early communication

During the past 30 years there have been dramatic advances in our understanding of infant development, and in the study of early communication between infants and those who care for them. This has been partly due to the advent of video-recording, allowing the behaviour of adults and babies to be captured on film and then analysed frame by frame. The research findings show the extraordinary sensitivity and sophistication of the responses between infants and adults from the earliest days (Wood 1988). Far from being relatively passive, indifferent to their environment, very young babies are seen to initiate and engage in the subtlest forms of contact with their caretakers, synchronising their movements, demonstrating from birth an 'intention' to explore and respond to the aspects of their environment. Of course, in the early weeks the intentions are barely recognisable as such. Purpose and control need the maturing experience of time and practice to develop into competence. However, it is now clear that babies rapidly develop the ability to distinguish between sounds and sights and to respond selectively to them. Within a very short time babies can tell the difference between their mother's face and voice and that of others, and show distress or pleasure according to the expression on her face or the tone of her voice. Whereas in times past we believed it did not matter too much who handled babies, or how they were looked at or spoken to so long as it was with reasonable care, we now understand that it does, that babies are aware and that babies mind. However, despite 'knowing', 'feeling' and 'minding', babies in a relatively helpless position when it comes to communicating these feelings. They are dependent on the adult's ability to recognise and interpret any communication expressed through crying, gazing, smiling, and through the movements of arms and hands (Wood 1988).

Infants also begin to become aware of themselves and their separateness from others through the response to their actions. Dr Anthony Storr talks about the notion of 'self' growing out of the early interactions between the baby and the mother or mother substitute, and that it is the extension and expansion of contacts with others throughout their lives that provides people with a sense of self, and an inner coherence. He quotes the psychiatrist Heinz Kohut on the importance of the relationships between the baby and the parent-figures at this early stage. Kohut said that adults need to reinforce the child's sense of self through recognising and mirroring the child's developing identity *as it actually is,* empathising with the child's feelings, responding to the child's demands with *'non-hostile firmness and non-seductive affection'.* In other words, being firm without being rejecting and not becoming a slave to the baby's demands. Kohut believed that great damage is done to children's later development where parents are unable to provide this *'empathic understanding'.* As Storr explains, developing this sense of self is like looking in a mirror: a clear and polished mirror repeatedly reflects the developing person as they actually are, thus giving them a firm and true sense of their own identity; a cracked, dirty, smeared mirror provides the child with an inaccurate and distorted picture (Storr 1988).

These insights and perceptions into the behaviour of infants and the growth of personality have a particular significance for the study of exceptional children's development. We may still be unsure as to the relative importance of genetic inheritance and physical and social environment in making us who we are and in bringing about the differences between us, but even so, we can assume that we are born with differing response patterns. Any parent, or any person who has closely observed newborn infants, knows that this is so. We need, in fact, claim no more than this: to be born with different response patterns inevitably sets off a train of reciprocal relationships that ensures unique development.

Response to the environment

One could speculate that children who later develop their abilities to exceptional levels are born with a highly sensitised capacity to respond to their environment. Learning is all about experiencing. It is through our contact with our world that we grow to know our world and to develop our capacity to 'think' about it and to organise ourselves within it. A child born with highly sensitive response mechanisms is likely to experience more and be more aware of the surrounding environment than an infant with slower or more muted receptivity. This may or may not show itself in a greater restlessness or apparent alertness. Some quiet babies may also be taking in a great deal more than others.

Whether or not there is a genetic component to the way babies respond to early experiences may be of great interest to those concerned with the academic study of human psychology. It is of much less importance to those whose business is *living* with children. What is important for them is the ability to understand what the consequences of such a possibility might be. It could mean, for instance, that highly sensitised infants might perceive sounds, images and physical sensations more acutely. Their reactions to events may be therefore stronger and more complex. This in turn has implications for the way in which parents create a stimulating environment for their child while safeguarding them from excessive stress.

Protecting the early relationship

Taking on responsibility for a new baby is one of the greatest challenges of all. It is a privilege and a joy, but it can also be an anxious time because we know that the first two years of a baby's life set the foundations for future growth. An adequate level of physical care is essential for the healthy development of the child's body and mind but the *quality* of parenting will have a significant impact on the child's personality and psychological well-being. We know that babies who are socially neglected or who receive too little stimulation become listless and apathetic. Babies who are actively encouraged to explore their new world tend to develop more active and inquisitive minds. Babies are also very sensitive to the emotional atmosphere. Although they may not be able to explain their feelings, they do respond to the feelings of those around them. The baby whose behaviour irritates the parent will sense it and some important messages will begin to be communicated – messages of anger and frustration, of helplessness, of wishing to be free from the demands of child-care. Subconsciously the baby will begin to recognise and absorb these feelings and this may set a pattern for developing relationships which will affect the child's emotional health. There is even some evidence arising out of recent research into post-natal depression that difficulties in the early stages of parent–child relationships can have long-term repercussions on the family. It would appear that even very young babies can detect when adults are depressed, irritable or feel very low, and they too then become less sociable and withdrawn. So it makes sense to avoid wherever possible the sources of stress which are harmful to early relationships, and do whatever we can to create an environment that provides the security and welcome in which the baby's personality can flourish.

In the first two years of a young child's life the prime concern for the family is to adjust to the new living arrangements and to develop satisfactory and rewarding relationships. Adjusting to a new lifestyle is never easy but for the great majority of families this is an exciting and enriching period of their lives. For some, however, the situation is less happy. Parents can become confused and distressed when the new baby places demands on them that are greater than they had expected. They may have to think carefully about how they can ensure that the baby does not receive negative 'messages' which might damage future relationships or the baby's growing understanding about itself.

Exploration and play

In order to learn about the world the baby must explore it. In the earliest days while they are still relatively helpless, babies explore their surroundings with their eyes. Later, as control over movement develops and coordination becomes increasingly refined, the exploration will be extended through all the other senses: touching, banging, squeezing, shaking, tasting. By such means the child learns to 'know' the world around them and begins to learn the properties of the objects within it. Play is a way of further exploring and then testing what is being learned. Exploration and play are essential ingredients of both physical and intellectual growth. But, at times, parents can find the process rather exhausting.

As adults we love to watch babies becoming more skilful. We watch eagerly for each new sign of progress. We identify with the child's pleasure in each new experience and share the excitement and surprise as new things are discovered. This sharing of experience between adult and child is perhaps the most crucial and significant element in early human experience and one that will lay the foundations for all future relationships. Without a caring and participating adult, children will undoubtedly still explore the world around them because as human beings we have an innate drive to explore and to 'know' our environments. But, as was mentioned earlier, it is in the mirror of the adult's face that the child learns to interpret the new-found knowledge and to attach significance to it. In his book on the development of children's thinking Professor David Wood describes the complex interplay between mothers and their infants, where through eye contact and eye pointing they direct their baby's attention to objects and experiences in the environment, and then by describing and commenting on what is being observed, they provide a language and a meaning for the child's experience (Wood 1988).

Children react to each new skill they master, not only in terms of the immediate effect it has on them, but also in the effect it produces in others. Pleasure expressed by the adult evokes pleasure and satisfaction in the child. The two share the delight of a new discovery, of a new skill developing. The growth of understanding and skills becomes associated with the joy of love between human beings. Where this growth of skill and knowledge through exploration is not matched or mirrored by a human response, it remains as mere knowledge: objective, practical, impersonal. It may be that it is in the quality of these shared experiences, from the earliest moments of life, that future attitudes to learning and relationships are determined.

Play and exploration are instinctive and universal needs. However, in some children the drive to explore is so urgent and so excessive that their families are overwhelmed. Eager, restless, inquisitive babies and toddlers whose very energy may result in their absorbing their world at such a rate that their development becomes 'exceptional' can take their caretakers by surprise. In the early months such children can become intensely frustrated by the mismatch between the need to explore and their ability to satisfy their desire. Such children see or know what they want to do, but cannot physically manage to achieve it, or, if they do, cause chaos and destruction in the doing. We all know of children who are into everything. No sooner is your back turned than televisions, videos and electronic gadgets are turned on, objects pulled from every drawer and cupboard, and unexpected and disastrous uses found for precious possessions.

Oliver

'I was almost driven to despair,' said Oliver's mother. 'He was such a destructive child. From tiny, his main interest in any toy or object was to take it apart, if necessary with a hammer. Everything he touched was reduced to bits. At times I would shout and rage at him. It never seemed worth giving him any presents.' As Oliver grew older and the destruction extended remorselessly throughout the house, the relationship with his mother and sister became increasingly strained.

It is very hard indeed to remain calm in the face of such unrelenting enthusiasm and energy – very difficult to share the pleasure of the child's new-found skills. It is also extremely tiring. Ingenuity and a sense of humour are essential. Adults need to recognise and accept that children's desire to explore is instinctive and natural, and that, when very young, they will not be able to respond to 'reason'. Continuing to explore, despite their parents' displeasure, is not being naughty. Naughtiness is deliberate disobedience – an intention to disregard an instruction or to do deliberate damage. Babies cannot 'intend' in this way: their thinking is too primitive. Young children's need to explore must be satisfied if deep frustration and later depression are to be avoided. The more eager and inquisitive the child, the more potential there is for frustration for both parents and child, and the greater the need there will be for careful organisation and supervision to ensure that the child can explore safely.

Play offers the adult and child a precious opportunity to set the foundations for learning on human grounds; this is the foundation for sharing, communicating and negotiating. Play helps establish the boundaries of reciprocal loving relationships. It is vital that this foundation is a loving one. If, through the exercising of their natural desires, children encounter disapproval and anger, they will become confused. Curiosity and a zest for life will become associated with adult disapproval and anger. The consequences for future learning and future relationships are obvious. If, on the other hand, children's discoveries are complemented by the adult's pleasure, then discovery becomes a human joy, a means of experiencing shared adventures which establishes a template for future learning.

The preschool years

Early development of self-concept

The period of near-complete dependency, from the moment of birth to the time when the child becomes physically and emotionally able to explore beyond the environment of the home, is the foundation stage for healthy future development. This crucial period is normally characterised by the synchronisation of physical, intellectual and emotional growth. As physical strength and coordination increase, so too do the opportunities for exploration and therefore for learning. New experiences bring new awareness both of the physical world and of relationships with other human beings.

Moving out into the world brings with it exciting new opportunities for growth, but also increased possibilities of stress, particularly for children whose development is in any way unusual. This may certainly be the case for children whose physical and intellectual development are markedly out of phase, where, for instance, the child's physical development has proceeded normally, but where intellectual development is delayed; or where the child's intellectual development or physical development is exceptionally precocious.

As we have seen, learning about ourselves begins from the moment of birth. Throughout our lives we continue to learn about ourselves from the encounters we have with others. It is in the reflections of these encounters that we come to think of ourselves as clever or stupid, good or bad, kind or cruel. One unfortunate result of this process of learning is that some children can grow up thinking badly about themselves because of a history of unhappy encounters.

By living and growing together people also develop a shared understanding of what is 'normal'. In children, at certain stages of growth, certain skills are expected to emerge and develop within given age ranges. Thus, in our western society, we expect that babies will begin to babble and practise sound patterns during the first year. We anticipate that some words will become intelligible from 9 months onwards, and that these words will then be put together in simple sentences between 18 months and $2^1/_2$ years. We also expect babies to begin to sit up before their first birthday, to crawl any time between 9 and 15 months, and to walk by the time they are 18 months. These are the 'milestones' of early development and are watched for with interest by all concerned. Similar progress is expected in children's ability to use their hands in manipulating objects and in their response to events.

Awareness of these shared understandings becomes more apparent when a child's development surpasses our expectations. An infant who learns to put reasonable and intelligible sentences together before the age of 12 months is unusual. So is the child who, with no formal teaching, learns to read by the age of 2. We still do not understand why or how such skills can develop so early, but their appearance at this age will certainly cause surprise. Whether or not this is a problem lies not in the precocity itself but in how people respond. It is the way in which others respond, particularly adults, that will convey feelings of approval and reassurance, or disapproval and rejection. Very young children do not have the ability to reflect on their behaviour. They will, however, register the feelings that their presence and unself-conscious actions provoke in others. The children will certainly feel bewildered. Even from the earliest age, mixed messages, ambivalent feelings and unpredictable responses cause greater distress to small children than any straightforward expressions of anger.

What might be the implications for such children when their experience of people and activities widens beyond the immediate family? How might others respond? After all, it is surprising to meet a child of two who speaks like a five-year-old, or who can read fluently. It does take one aback to see a four-year-old writing complex adventure stories or demonstrating advanced mathematical understanding. It can be difficult not to express amazement at the obvious skills of infant artists or musicians. The danger is that from such reactions children can learn to think of themselves as 'extraordinary', someone special, someone who is superior to others. Believing that one is abnormal (in whatever sense) is a powerful isolator.

While most highly intelligent or talented children may excite comment, an unfortunate few may also be encouraged to perform in front of others, like circus creatures, to demonstrate their skills and receive applause. Such circumstances may encourage children to develop attitudes and behaviour that further isolate and alienate them. This was clearly the case with the little girl Katie, described on pages 2–3. In Joan Freeman's fascinating longitudinal study a number of the adults identified as 'gifted' when children felt they had been badly damaged by being put on show. 'I was emotionally scarred by being made to perform,' said Jeremy (Freeman 2001). It is, of course, not a question of denying the talents of a child or pretending that they do not possess the skills they so evidently have; it is rather a question of encompassing the skills within the framework of the child's 'normality'. Children, whatever the characteristics of their development, should be taken for who they are, not for how they compare to others.

If adults are aware of the power of the messages being conveyed to children at this stage then much greater care can be given to the way unusual development is encountered. Parents of children with unusual talents or abilities must do what they can to forestall the surprised reactions of others. Parents can forewarn relatives and friends. They can ensure that nothing is said to the children that will suggest to them that they are 'abnormal'. Any particular talents children possess should be accepted and enjoyed alongside all the other aspects of behaviour, no more, no less. Children must be allowed to develop a sense of belonging and of being 'as others', as well as enjoying the feeling of being unique, and special. No child should feel that their need to be loved and valued is won through the display of talents. They should never be put on show. An American writer with much experience of exceptional children observed:

> The most important thing the world can give to the gifted child is a welcome and an acknowledgement of their human as well as their intellectual capacities. While this is a need all children share, the gifted child's own accomplishments, by being outstanding, may work to his own detriment, if they alone are the means by which his world acknowledges him. (Vail 1979)

Relating to other children

It may be very difficult to help the exceptional child to form relationships with other children. While they are still very small, contacts with other young children depend very much on the sociability of the parents and how often they meet together with other adults and their children. Very young children tend to play *alongside* rather than *with* each other. Nevertheless, from very early on we can see the beginnings of shared play, with the taking and offering of play-objects between one another. Even at this early play stage, it is also noticeable that the behaviour of some children affects that of others. Personal styles are already quite well marked. Some young children are energetic and forceful; others are more cautious. Dominant and sturdy-minded children with a boisterous style of approach can be seen to shock and distress their more timid companions. They seem, literally, to launch themselves upon the newcomer: hair is pulled, eyes are poked at, toys are snatched away. Great excitement and pleasure is usually shown by the aggressor during these encounters; less by the victim. When children are very young, the situations are usually resolved by adults: children are separated, consoled, reprimanded; toys are restored to rightful owners and new diversions found.

As a child grows older contacts with other children become more frequent, and more play takes place between the children themselves. They spend longer together and evolve more of the activities themselves. Very bright children and their parents may welcome the additional source of exploration and interest such experiences provide. They may be eager to make use of other resources such as toddler groups, playgroups or nursery classes. A wider network of social contacts and the opportunities for exploration and new learning may be just what is needed to satisfy the bright child's eager curiosity.

For most children this is so, and the new stage in the family's situation is a happy and rewarding one. For a few, however, it may be rather more problematical. Many parents recount how difficult it was to integrate their child into the play of other toddlers. Play is a complex activity, with its own developmental stages and styles. Children can play on their own; they can also play with others. Where play is a shared activity, its success depends on some common agreements and shared understandings among those involved. At the simplest, most primitive level, this calls upon skills of cooperation, adaptability and compromise, the 'give-and-take' transactions.

The problem for very bright or precocious children is that they are often, intellectually at least, several steps ahead of their peers in terms of their play interests; they are often operating at a more sophisticated level. Such children start playing with another child or with a group of children, but quickly become impatient with the activities. They want to take over the leadership, alter the game sequence, redefine the rules. Emotionally they may be no more mature than their companions, so when they are frustrated they may throw tantrums or try to wreck other children's activities. The result is misery for everyone concerned. Bright children may be enormously disappointed with their efforts to play with others. They may want to join in but the play on offer bores or frustrates them. They cannot understand why *they* do not understand and may learn to think that their playmates are 'stupid'. In turn, the other children are likely to resent the destruction of the rhythm of their own play. No-one likes being made to feel stupid. As a result they avoid contact with the discomfort-making child and they may reject them from the group.

What often happens next is the precocious child tries to join a group of older children. However, this is not always successful. Older children often resent the intrusion. They will either use the child as a butt for their own play or find it amusing to encourage behaviour that gets the child into trouble. Either way, the precocious child is not included in a friendship group and may continue to disrupt the activities of others, or retreat to the safer world of home. There the child can defend themselves from the misery of rejection by dismissing others as not being worth the trouble, and concentrating on activities that will bring the comfort of adult approval. Such children experience a distressing split in their lives: wanting to play and join with others; finding it frustrating and confusing when they do so. They are unable to find a satisfactory way round the relationship problem so they often turn to knowledge to fill the gap. They discover that they can restrict their explorations to intellectual discoveries. They learn to depend on adults for approval, and to gain this through intellectual prowess. Play provides the opportunity to learn how to engage with others, but it is also the area where the rejection of the child who lacks the appropriate social skills is exposed.

Considerable tact and creative thinking by adults are needed to handle such situations. It may be a question of trying to achieve some kind of compromise. Parents may need to be actively, though tactfully, involved in helping the child develop relationships, looking for occasions where the child can take part comfortably in a group of others of a similar age, as well as for opportunities to develop interests at the child's own intellectual level. They will need to help create situations in which the taking part does not depend on everyone having the same level of ability.

There are lots of opportunities for children to find ways of enjoying doing things together within the home itself and in the immediate surroundings of most neighbourhoods: helping with the cooking and shopping; painting and modelling; games of make-believe; physical activities and visits to places of local interest. Where children experience difficulty in managing their contact with others on their own, adults can ease the way by first inviting just one child to share a supervised activity or 'treat' outing, and then, as relationships develop, either by extending the time of contact or the range of activities. More children can be added to form a larger group. So long as the precocious child has contact with others of a similar age and some experience of taking part with them in some mutually rewarding activity, then the foundations for constructive relationships will be maintained. It is also important for precocious children to be able to share interests and experiences at their own intellectual level. Here it may be necessary to look for others with similar interests, even older children or adults, and to bring them together from time to time. The National Association for Gifted Children (NAGC) and the association for Children of High Intelligence (CHI) provide a service for children and their families.

Parental management

The period that is sometimes called the 'terrible twos' can often be a difficult stage for parents to manage. Children are becoming aware of their growing competence and independence and begin to challenge their parents' authority. It is the stage of the dramatic 'No's' and the temper tantrums. Small children, caught up in the fierceness of their desires and their frustration at being prevented from immediately gratifying them, are often overwhelmed by the strength of their feelings. Their little bodies literally tremble and shake with the force of their passions. Some psychologists suggest that children may sometimes even be afraid that the sheer intensity of their anger will destroy the object of their rage. Parents must be able to reassure their children that no matter how angry or how bad the feelings are, they can be managed and contained. Once the boundaries have been tested and found to hold, children are then safe to continue to explore.

One of the major problems for intellectually precocious children is that they may feel insecure during this period. They gain glimpses of their parents' weakness or uncertainty at a time when emotionally they cannot cope with anything less than parental infallibility. A number of adolescents who remember this period describe consciously 'outwitting' their parents, of feeling scornful of their parents' confusion and distress. The youngsters talk of the shock of discovering at this early age the ability to manipulate adults. Their world felt fundamentally insecure. If one has the care of such a child, it is most important to remember at all times that, however demanding and angry the child becomes, however clever and persuasive the child's arguments might be, young children need to find that the parents *are* in control and will protect them from themselves. What all children need above all is to find that the world is safe and that it can withstand their onslaughts. It is important for parents to be clear in their minds as to what they feel is right, what should happen, when and how, and to follow their decisions through, calmly but firmly. Good parenting for all children requires sensitive but firm management. Very bright and able children are no exception.

This chapter has concentrated on some of the difficulties that may arise when a young child's development is precocious. There is no doubt that some young children present real challenges to the skills, energy and patience of those who care for them. While there may be problems and uncertainties this can be a wonderful stage in a parent's relationship with a child. It offers the adult the opportunity and privilege of returning to rediscover the wonder of one's surroundings, to look again at things previously taken for granted and to share in real excitement with the innocent delight of a child. The secret of sustaining the pleasure lies in the willingness to join the children at their level, to understand their need to explore, to provide a wide range of suitable learning opportunities and to respond sensitively to the inevitable frustrations when they find they cannot do everything they want.

Adults need to call upon their own ingenuity and also on the experience of others. There are many useful books and other resources on the market which help parents play an active role in their children's early learning (see Reference sections). In particular, Joan Freeman's books *Bright as a Button* and *How to Raise a Bright Child* provide a wealth of ideas for encouraging language, perception, early number concepts, interests in scientific investigations and creative thinking. Many of the suggestions are creative, practical and relatively simple to organise. The emphasis is on the need for children to work towards their own solutions and create their own unique experiences (Freeman 1991, 1991a, 1995).

CHAPTER 4

Starting school

Establishing the partnership

It takes a whole village to raise a child.

(Akan proverb)

David and Sarah were nearly five when I first met them. David was about to start school and his parents were worried about the way his new teachers would respond to his difficult behaviour. Sarah had already been admitted early to her infant school at her parents' request as she was understood to be exceptionally bright. David's parents and Sarah's head teacher had both contacted me for advice. Here were two different problems presented from two different perspectives, but together they illustrate some of the most commonly encountered sources of difficulty at this important stage in children's development.

David

David had been a difficult child from birth. As a baby he was very restless. He walked early, explored relentlessly and had kept his parents constantly on their toes. He had shown little sense of danger, climbing all over the furniture, jumping from alarming heights, experimenting with whatever came to hand. By the age of 2 he was already showing an interest in reading. He had started to recognise signs, and soon began identifying articles by their labels both in the home and in shops. He seemed to 'understand' the process without being taught. When David was offered a place at the local playgroup his parents were delighted. They welcomed the chance of a break from the constant supervision, and felt he would enjoy the additional stimulation of group activities. Their pleasure was short-lived.

David's exuberant behaviour was not appreciated by the children, or by the playgroup supervisors. Complaints escalated. Soon David's mother began to dread the moment she went to collect him each morning. Almost inevitably some incident would be mentioned to her. She was aware that the word was being spread among the mothers of other children in the group and that she was being criticised for her failure to control her child. His behaviour was affecting the way she was being judged as a person. She was also aware of a feeling of disapproval from playgroup staff that David could read. She sensed that they thought she was pressuring the child to satisfy her own ambitions. Her explanations had been listened to politely but with scepticism. She was warned that both David's unruly behaviour and his precocity would be bound to cause difficulties at his new school. In short, David's parents were encouraged to feel thoroughly anxious, especially about the prospect of his starting school.

Figure 4.1 David's exuberant behaviour was not appreciated

Sarah

Sarah's parents, on the other hand, had requested an early admission to school. They had told the head teacher that she was exceptionally bright, was already reading fluently and able to write independently. They felt she needed the structure of school to satisfy her intellectual curiosity. The head teacher was a little reluctant, but finally agreed to admit Sarah when she was only four. A week after she started school, Sarah's parents returned to talk to the class teacher. The child, the parents said, was unhappy. She was apparently disappointed with what was being offered and frustrated by the lack of 'real' work. She was bored by spending so much time in play activities. She wanted to write and do sums, and did not like having to play with sand and water. Sarah's parents wanted to know what the class teacher was doing in the way of formal teaching, and asked to see the children's workbooks. Not unnaturally the teacher felt threatened by such a questioning approach. Defensive attitudes were struck by both sides.

The start of formal schooling is the first and probably most crucial educational transition point. It is a particularly sensitive time for parents and children. Of course many will have used child-care services, or the child may have attended a playgroup or a nursery school. For them, the start of formal schooling may be easier as the process of separation and the sharing of the responsibility of care is more gradual. Nevertheless, the start of formal schooling is an important milestone. It signals explicitly and emphatically that the responsibility for the care and upbringing of a child is a community venture: a responsibility in which parents have the major role, but one where others make an increasingly important contribution. Some parents may find this hard to accept and a source of anxiety. This is especially likely if their child's development is in any way unusual.

Sharing the care of their child also presents parents with a new perspective on their own identity. They are faced, perhaps for the first time in their lives, with the unavoidable fact that they will be judged not only on how *they* behave or on the relationships that they themselves are able to establish, but also on the behaviour and social skills of their child: they are judged by the way their child behaves. This is an alarming realisation for most people. Small wonder so much effort goes into ensuring that children conform to socially accepted forms of behaviour!

Parents may also find themselves, again perhaps for the first time, in a situation where they realise that they are not the only experts as far as their child is concerned. As the circle widens, and other people begin to be involved, new knowledge and understandings about the child's personality, capabilities and needs begin to develop. The parents' perspectives become only part of the picture. Sometimes their views and opinions may be questioned or, worse, not believed. Whatever the case, parents will naturally feel apprehensive about their first encounters with school and teachers, and may wonder whether their child's needs will be recognised and treated with sensitivity. Where both parties, parents and school staff, handle these early relationships with care and tact, there is usually a smooth transition to the new environment. Where people become defensive, this can work against the best interests of the child. It is vital at this stage for schools and parents to work in partnership to resolve, rather than dismiss, whatever anxieties each might feel.

Partnership with parents is now very much on the agenda for all schools, particularly since the implementation of the 1994 Code of Practice for children with special educational needs. Schools are required to have in place effective strategies for keeping in touch with parents, and for providing regular and detailed information about their child's progress. Such practice is often best in nursery and primary phase schools where it is easier to meet on a regular basis, but it is vital that, right from the start, parents and schools develop an expectation of a partnership which will carry through to the rest of the child's education. Partnership, of course, is not always easy to achieve, depending as it does on hard work, understanding and trust. It can only develop where all those concerned wish to share their experiences and are prepared to demonstrate to one another that they value the varied skills and contributions each brings to the relationship.

In the cases of David and Sarah the situations were resolved once both parents and school were able to see how much could be gained from trusting cooperation. David's new teacher invited his parents to share with her the kinds of difficulties they had faced in managing his excessive energy, and to advise her on how best to respond to his need to boss around other children. Together they agreed on a policy with regard to handling the child and to meeting regularly to see that all was going well. They were able to discuss David's advanced reading skills, and consider what kind of balance should be sought between the development of basic skills and the need to provide all the other vital experiences of shared play and creative work.

Sarah's situation was a little more complex but also had a happy outcome. The main difficulty was the lack of appreciation between parents and teacher of each other's points of view. Once they had shared their respective thoughts and experiences, many areas of agreement were reached. Sarah's teacher was able to explain the philosophy behind her approach and to validate the activities that Sarah's parents had dismissed as 'play'. She was able to offer the parents a view of the child's needs in terms of relating to other children in a way they had not been able to appreciate before. The teacher told their parents that she herself had never met a child with such advanced reading and writing skills at this age, and admitted that this presented her with a real professional challenge. Sarah's parents, once they believed that their child's special abilities were recognised and taken seriously, were able to consider sympathetically the problems faced by the teacher, and conceded that Sarah's frustrations were probably due more to social upsets than lack of intellectual challenge in the class. Instead of criticising they offered to help where possible. They agreed to keep in touch about what Sarah was doing at home so that the teacher knew on what interests to build and which to reinforce. They also offered their own support for school activities.

Both David and Sarah were lucky enough to have parents and teachers who were honest enough to admit to each other their mutual need for advice. As a result, though their lives in school were not without their difficult moments, they both continued to do well, remaining active and enthusiastic and becoming accepted among their peers, despite their obvious exceptional abilities.

Choosing a school

All parents want their children to go to a school where they will be happy and where they will receive an education that fosters and develops their abilities and meets their individual needs. For many parents choosing a school for their child is not a realistic option. House location, school catchment areas, local education policies, school admission policies and transport facilities may all determine to which school the child will go. Even parents who appear to have a choice may nevertheless find themselves unable to obtain their preference because of local circumstances and individual school arrangements. In many instances, where there is competition for places, schools choose the pupils and parents rather than the other way round. The whole process can be very stressful.

Whether or not there is a choice, it is important that parents find out as much as possible about the schools to which their child may be going, before their child is admitted. Where the child's development is in any way unusual, it is particularly important to find out about the school's attitudes towards 'individual needs' and about any special provision that may be offered. The National Association for Able Children in Education (NACE) has published a useful pamphlet to help parents prepare for the things they might look for and the questions they might ask on their initial visit (NACE Parent Leaflet No. 1). The pamphlet suggests that parents should have ready any evidence they have to support their belief that their child may need special attention. They should ask:

- what arrangements the school makes to identify and take note of children's special abilities
- how teachers plan for different levels of work within the same class
- what extra opportunities are provided to extend more able pupils
- how flexible are the arrangements for grouping pupils
- what use the school makes of facilities and people outside the school.

When looking round the school and classrooms parents should take note of the range of books and equipment as well as the display of children's work.

Most importantly, they should try to judge the 'feel' of the school: whether there is a lively and pleasurable 'buzz' in classrooms and whether the children seem to be interested in their work, enjoying the activities and working cooperatively. The 'ethos' of the school and the way a school responds to both parents and children can tell parents a lot about how confident they can be that their child's needs will be taken into account. Evidence that teachers and children are enjoying what they are doing, a positive response from the head teacher to parents' interests and concerns, and a willingness to discuss any special attention that may be needed are important indicators of a school that pays proper regard to children's welfare and development.

The early years

Balancing intellectual, emotional and social needs

Some children can enter school at the age of 5 with skills so precocious that the teacher is unsure how best to structure their learning. If a child already reads and writes fluently, or demonstrates mathematical competence way beyond their years, the early years teacher may doubt whether he or she has the experience or the resources to meet the child's needs. How, for instance, does the teacher build upon existing knowledge and skills while at the same time ensuring that the learning experiences are appropriate for the child's emotional stage of development?

Rebecca

Rebecca, started school when she was 4 years 2 months. Her reading ability, according to a test of reading skill, was similar to that of a 12-year-old. Not only could she read fluently, but she also clearly understood most of what she read. She was able to alter the inflexion of her voice to mark changes in the events of the narrative, and to give sensible definitions for the more difficult words.

Teachers are clearly faced with a problem in a situation such as this, if only at the level of providing appropriate reading materials. Careful thought has to be given to the kind of books young children read. A child must be allowed access to a full and varied reading experience, but the ideas and the information children encounter should also be suitable for the stage of their emotional growth and their ability to respond in feeling as well as in intellectual terms. Some books that children might technically be able to read are quite unsuitable in terms of content, since they are written to meet the interests of young adolescents. Books written specifically for children of

Rebecca's age were of limited interest to her and lacked the breadth and richness of vocabulary she enjoyed. However, it is not always necessary to see progress in reading as the ability to read ever more demanding texts. On the contrary, it is often more appropriate for children to be encouraged to use a simple story as the basis for a range of creative activities. This might include expanding and elaborating the theme through writing or recording, researching stories that have similar events or characters or writing a play on a similar theme. The able child is often just as excited by extending, enriching and transforming material as by acquiring new knowledge. It is certainly possible even at this early stage to help children become skilful at selecting resources and reading materials to satisfy their interests and further their own learning. In situations such as Rebecca's it is essential that teacher and parent consult together and decide jointly what is the best approach.

A similar dilemma can be faced when a child starts school with precocious mathematical ability. Teachers tend to be wary of unusual mathematical skills at this stage. They may suspect that the ability to manipulate figures may not be matched by a proper conceptual understanding. They can also be anxious about their own ability to provide adequately for such children, and worried that parents may begin to question their competence. Ian, for example, was a child who showed an advanced ability with numbers from a very early age. By the age of 4 he was able to manipulate numbers to 100 and enjoyed making up his own mathematical puzzles and games. His father, who was a teacher of mathematics in a secondary school, enjoyed playing 'maths' activities with his son in the evening and at weekends. Ian's parents visited the school before the child was admitted and were keen to know what his teacher would do to build on his interest and skills. She, not unexpectedly, felt rather anxious and said that she would want to ensure that his knowledge and understanding were securely grounded before introducing more advanced work. Such an approach may be entirely appropriate.

Some children, even when very young, acquire the ability to do calculations and see the answers to problems very quickly, apparently skipping the stages in the process that most others need to follow. Teachers need to know what a child is doing, and how and why answers are being found, in order to identify any faults in the logic or the understandings which might affect later learning. Children also need to learn how to explain what they are doing and to develop successful learning strategies. To do this they may need to rehearse and practise particular routines. However, even with young children, teachers' anxieties or lack of understanding of how to explore topics in a wide variety of ways may mean that the same exercises are followed and practised by all the children in the class, even when this means a very able child rehearsing routines with which they are completely familiar. This can lead to boredom and frustration. Far better to provide children with opportunities to be creative with their existing skills, and to encourage them to look for new ways of finding solutions and calculating answers by exploring new sequences and patterns. There are now many excellent resources to help teachers provide a wide range of mathematical activities for able children of all ages, including the use of the internet (see Reference sections).

Teaching and learning in science can sometimes present similar dilemnas. Fortunately, with the advent of the National Curriculum as a framework for learning, teachers now have a much clearer guide for their planning and teaching. The breadth of mathematical and scientific experience required by the programmes of study provides sufficient potential challenge for most children at this early age. Nevertheless, there will be some exceptional children whose speed of learning and levels of skills and understanding could present problems even to reasonably experienced teachers and they will need to seek advice from friends and colleagues. It may also be necessary to consult with teachers of older children, or to look for help from interested adults in the community (this is discussed further in Chapter 12).

Teachers of children with precocious intellectual development must also be mindful of the need to safeguard the balance in their learning experiences, and ensure that all children have appropriate opportunities to foster their social and emotional development. Sometimes parents of very able children put greater value on their need to make progress in formal aspects of their learning and undervalue the importance of play and social learning. Rebecca's parents were worried that she would spend too much of her time during the first year of school 'playing' rather than developing her academic talents. Initially they were unconvinced by the school's emphasis on Rebecca's need to spend as much time on unstructured activities as she did on more formal work. Nor did they accept the school's account of the broader learning opportunities that such activities provided. They suspected that this was more to do with the teacher's uncertainty about how to handle the child's advanced skills. But play is an essential part of the learning process. It allows the child to explore and experiment, to discover the dynamics of cause and effect, to build imaginary worlds, to rehearse new roles, to practise new skills away from the direction and control of adults. Play is the basis for early social relationships, where children learn to share and to cooperate. By the age of 5, children's play has become a complex and sophisticated process where they are learning not only with but also from each other. A child who has not learned to play is seriously at risk. If parents are worried about their children 'playing' in school this must be openly discussed so that the purpose and the value to the child are more readily appreciated.

Helping reduce frustration

There are other problems arising from mismatch within a young child's pattern of development, or between a child and the social environment, that call upon not so much the professional competence of a teacher, but upon a teacher's sensitivity. Exceptionally intelligent children are liable to suffer terrible frustrations, particularly when they are very young and their physical coordination is as yet immature, or when they are unable to achieve their goals. The problem is that they so often know what it is they want to do, but lack the physical ability to achieve it. This is often most apparent in the areas of writing, and practical and constructional skills.

Learning to write is itself a laborious business. It requires care, patience and reasonable coordination. For very young children it can be a highly unsatisfactory way of expressing thoughts and ideas, rarely producing what was intended. Young children's ability to express their thinking is limited not so much by the quality of the ideas as by the physical difficulty of guiding the pen across the page. Unfortunately, the process of writing transforms the potentially exciting communication of ideas into a struggle between the pen and paper and the child. The greater the wealth of ideas and the desire to communicate, the greater the frustration. Sensitivity is all-important in understanding how such frustration affects very intelligent and imaginative children. Alongside formal writing instruction and practice, such children need to be offered a wide variety of opportunities for sharing their interests and plans. It is, of course, important that ideas be given physical expression, that they be recorded in ways in which children can 'own' them, and with pride. The rapid advance in the use of information and communication technology, with the access this provides to the use of graphics and illustration, has provided a whole new world of possibilities for teachers and for children. This is likely to help overcome many of the difficulties that impede children's learning and create frustration, particularly for those who find difficulty with the early stages of writing.

Frustration caused by the inability to give proper expression to ideas reveals itself in other ways. Many teachers and parents will have encountered children who, even at a very young age, work at particular projects almost to the point of obsession. They appear to be driven by some inner dream, refusing to be influenced by the reassurance of others, insisting on working and reworking until the plan has been perfected. If they cannot create what they have in mind to a standard they deem acceptable, the offending object will often be suddenly rejected or violently and angrily destroyed. This desire for perfection can be a source of intense distress to children; it can also baffle and irritate those who have to care for them. With such children there is little to be gained by praising the work the child has rejected. If what the children have produced does not look right to them, then their opinions and feelings must be respected. We must bear in mind that such children depend as much on internal evaluation as on praise from others. Parents and teachers have to find ways of helping children achieve their aims, by carefully offering advice, by helping them with part of the task, and by reassuring them and helping them cope with failures when they occur.

The early years in school are a critical period in a child's life. They set a pattern for learning and social relationships that can affect the way children respond to school in the longer term. Developmental studies of children's concepts of friendship demonstrate the crucial importance, even for the very young school child, of social relationships. Children's sense of well-being, their motivation and de-motivation for learning and their willingness to take part in activities with others are deeply affected by what they believe other children think about them (Wood 1999). It is vitally important that these early experiences are well managed.

CHAPTER 5

The primary years

Human needs

Children spend a large proportion of their life in school. They go there to *learn* in the widest possible interpretation of the word. They learn about themselves, about being a person within a group of others, about the community in which they live, and about the world around them. The kind of learning that occurs, and how it is acquired, will determine the progress the children make and the understandings they develop about themselves and others. In other words it helps determine the kind of people they become.

Children learn best when they feel safe and secure. The principal task for schools and teachers is to create environments in which *all* children grow to be confident in themselves as learners and as people. Schools that are successful in developing such confidence are those which are able to build a 'community for learning'.

In order to develop this confidence children need to feel welcome and valued. Maslow, an American psychologist, provided a most useful structure for understanding the path to self-fulfilment and the ability to become what he termed a 'self-actualised' person, capable of building a rich and fulfilling life and of contributing to the greater good. He proposed that, as human beings, we have a hierarchy of needs, each level of which must be satisfied to a reasonable degree before a person is capable of progressing to a higher level. The model states that we all share the basic physical needs for food and shelter, and that we all need to have a reasonable measure of certainty and consistency in our environment, to love and be loved, to feel we belong and that others are interested in our welfare, to feel good about ourselves, and to develop a sense of purpose in our lives. When a particular level of need remains unsatisfied a person's energies continue to focus on that aspect of their life.

For instance, if children are malnourished and ill-cared for they will have little interest in anything other than finding comfort and food. If children's lives are full of distress and uncertainties and they are never sure who will be at home to look after them, they will spend much of their time seeking reassurance, and trying to establish some predictability in their lives.

The level of 'loving and being loved', being a valued member of a group, is the pivotal level in the hierarchy, *the* essential human need, which must be satisfied if children are to develop a positive view of themselves. The need is so great that if love and respect do not come easily and naturally from those around, then children will seek out other sources. They will find ways of gaining attention, soliciting affection, buying their way into a group. If these strategies fail to win them the interest and affection they crave, then many children will find alternative ways of seeking personal reassurance.

Table 5.1 Maslow's hierarchy of needs

Level 6   NEED FOR MEANING
Finding a meaning for life, a purpose for one's existence

⇑

Level 5   SELF-ACTUALISATION
Self-development, autonomy, challenge

⇑

Level 4   SELF-ESTEEM
Feeling good about oneself

⇑

Level 3   LOVING, BEING LOVED AND BELONGING
Being accepted, wanted and respected

⇑

Level 2   PSYCHOLOGICAL SAFETY
Feeling safe, being able to predict events, actions and consequences

⇑

Level 1   PHYSICAL NEEDS
Food, shelter, self-preservation, reproduction

For some children, 'growing up gifted' can be difficult, as Joan Freeman so ably describes in her book *Gifted Children Growing Up* (Freeman 1991b). Parents whose child's development is unusual may be unsure how best to manage their relationships or provide for their needs. It can also be challenging for the teachers responsible for providing suitable learning experiences. And it can be problematic for such children when they find that their interests and abilities set them apart from others of their age. The emergence of an unusual talent or ability is a challenge to us all. However, children with exceptional abilities still have the same fundamental needs as others. They need to be liked. They need people to respect them for who they are, more than for what they do. They need teachers to recognise their stage of development and their particular learning styles. They do best when they are given a balance of support, encouragement and challenge, and where they have opportunities to explore their learning and practise their skills in as wide a variety of settings as possible.

But exceptional ability brings with it many 'special' features that we need to remember when working out ways of living and learning together. Children with exceptional abilities can face particular difficulties in developing a sense of belonging, in having their needs recognised and in being offered learning opportunities that encourage and sustain their interest and excitement. Throughout their infancy and early childhood they may be made to feel 'special' through comments made about them and by responses to their behaviour. They can learn to think of themselves as 'more' than others – more skilful, more talented, more deserving of time and attention. Their precocious behaviour and interests may make other children, and adults, feel uncomfortable and this may reinforce their feeling of not belonging, of not being easy to be with. They can become 'Able Mis-fits', as Kellmer Pringle called them in her study of very able troubled children (Kellmer Pringle 1970).

Since feelings of belonging, of being loved and made welcome, and feeling good about oneself are so essential to our emotional well-being, 'unusual' children may resort to ways of having these needs satisfied that create further distance between themselves and others such as:

- they may seek the company of older children if children of their own age are found to be unsatisfactory companions, or they may court the attention of adults who will at least make them feel good about their accomplishments
- they may consciously limit their performance and disguise their abilities if their greater understanding, skill, or work rate causes difficulties with their peers
- they may try to gain attention by attempting to buy their way into the group, or to play the class clown
- they may decide that people are not worth the effort and that their own company and the solitary pursuit of their own interests are more rewarding.

None of these strategies is satisfactory for the child's well-being in the long term. A child should never be allowed to feel a 'misfit'. There should always be a way in which each child's uniqueness can be welcomed and their contribution valued. Some of these approaches are discussed in Chapter 9 on school organisation and provision.

Fostering relationships

During the primary years of schooling children spend much of their time within the physical environment of a particular classroom, with a particular group of children and with a particular teacher. The actual classroom or the teacher may change each year, but the class group is unlikely to do so. For those children who find themselves unacceptable to their peers, or in an unsatisfactory relationship with their teacher, life in school becomes a punishing experience.

Friends are essential at all stages of life. Without friends many of the activities we undertake are meaningless. People without friends are an exceptionally vulnerable group. Their health and welfare is constantly at risk. The ability to make and to retain friends is therefore a great gift and one that we should cherish and foster in all our children. As Joan Freeman's follow-up study of 210 gifted children has shown, the majority of children with exceptional abilities do establish satisfactory relationships (Freeman 2001). Where they do not, they may not do well in school and in later life, so we need to be prepared to intervene. This can be done in a number of ways, for instance:

- look for ways in which the child's particular talents can contribute to the work of the class or the group as a whole, and so be recognised and valued by others;
- organise activities that are known to be particularly popular where the friendless child is joined by a small group of other pupils who are keen to take part in the activity itself;
- discuss the situation openly and honestly with the class, and invite some pupils to form a 'Circle of Friends' who will agree to invite the child to join their games, and defend against any unkindness;
- create a Circle Time and work with the whole class to resolve interpersonal tensions or playground problems. This is a successful technique to facilitate the inclusion of all pupils within the community of the class;
- talk with the child and the family and explore ways in which the hostility or rejection can be lessened.

A school and a class that sets out quite explicitly to create this community ethos and shared responsibility for each other's welfare will create an environment in which problems with relationships can be resolved.

The relationship between child and teacher is key. Teaching is a skilled activity that requires a combination of training, ability and experience. However, at any moment teachers can find themselves faced with professional challenges for which their training and experience may not have been sufficient. This may well be the case where children present extreme demands in their learning or in their social relationships. It can also happen when a child's capacity to learn is way beyond that which is expected. In such situations teachers may feel inadequate and threatened.

Children who openly and repeatedly challenge the knowledge and competence of a teacher are unlikely to endear themselves, however much that teacher tries to remain sympathetic. It is not always possible to *like* everything about one's pupils, but it is possible and essential to show professional concern for every child's welfare and development. Where able children appear at times to challenge a teacher's expertise, their behaviour can possibly be based on a determination to establish facts, not on a desire to make the teacher look foolish. The teacher should respond firmly, acknowledge the right to question and recognise the possibility that anyone can make mistakes. By so doing children are then encouraged to see that learning is a shared enterprise, and to believe that their own contributions will be accepted and taken seriously.

Figure 5.1 'Please, Miss, shouldn't that be a six?'

Developing an appropriate self-concept and establishing positive attitudes to learning

Confidence in oneself as a learner grows not only through acknowledgement and praise for your efforts and achievements from people whose opinion you value, but also through being able personally to recognise your own success. Success in school is not always easy to ensure. Some children, particularly those who find difficulty with the early stages of learning to read and write, quickly lose confidence in themselves as potential 'learners'. One often hears such children, even very young ones, say, 'I'm no good at drawing', 'I can't do sums' or 'I don't write nicely'. It is as if they believe their current difficulties to be inherent disabilities that can never be overcome.

Very able or talented children will not usually face this particular problem. They may in fact find the acquisition of skills and the understanding of tasks all too easy. But continual experience of success can accustom children to believing that this is their right, that they will always be successful in whatever they choose to do. By finding they can do all that is asked without much effort, such children are in danger of developing an unrealistic sense of their own capabilities, a super-inflated confidence, which will be just as counter-productive to future learning as a lack of confidence. On the other hand, children who find that their unusual learning abilities and talents create hostile responses from others may steadily lose whatever confidence they originally possessed and begin to devalue themselves as learners.

For some children the constant need to maintain high-level performance at all times and throughout their school career can be an unwelcome burden, as Emma found out.

Emma

'What worries me,' I said, turning over page after page of Emma's work, 'is that you don't appear to have anything but top marks or comments such as "Very Good" or "Excellent". How would you feel if you were handed back something that was given a "B" grade or rated as merely "Good"?' 'Terrible,' said Emma, 'really awful. I'd feel I'd failed. I think I'd be ashamed or something, I'd have let myself down. I'd try and work twice as hard next time.' Emma was 13 and had begun to show signs of stress towards the end of her first year at secondary school. She spent hours each night on her homework, setting herself almost impossibly high standards. She would rewrite essays if there was so much as a single spelling mistake on a page. She withdrew from a tutorial class offered to pupils who their teachers believed would benefit from some additional intellectual challenge, for fear that missing a normal class for one hour a week might affect her marks. Emma needed the constant reaffirmation of her 'A'-grade rating.

Young people can become high-level performers in various ways. A few may be such rapid learners and able thinkers that they find it easy to produce high-quality work. For some, teachers' expectations of their abilities may be too low, and the work they set fails to challenge. But for others their performance is due to sheer hard work and a high level of motivation. Constant expectation of high-level performance may create a state of continual stress for the child. During the primary years in school the belief in themselves as 'high performers' can become embedded in their very self-concept, part of their fundamental '*me*'. To be faced with evidence that suggests otherwise is an attack on their sense of self and produces a feeling of acute anxiety and dismay. Children find it very difficult to separate themselves from the outcomes of their efforts. They believe that succeeding makes you worthwhile as a person, and failure is diminishing. They cannot necessarily understand that the inability to solve a problem depends as much on the nature of the problem as on the ability of the person attempting to resolve it. If children come to believe that their intelligence or their specific talent is their main, and perhaps their only, asset, then the need to cling on to this concept of themselves assumes a disproportionate importance. This is one of the reasons why some youngsters will often refuse to have a go at something they believe may be difficult.

The seeds of children's responses to the challenge of learning are sown in the primary years. If teachers and parents are not careful, this need to be a top performer at all times may become truly burdensome and have negative long-term consequences. For the high-performing children maintaining their image and work levels can become increasingly difficult as each year passes. For those who achieve their high standards through hard work and high levels of motivation the increasing demands of the secondary school curriculum can begin to pose a very real threat. In reality only children with outstanding talents will manage to sustain top-line performance throughout each year of their school career. Some children may accept this fact with equanimity; others may not. Children who feel the need to cling to a belief and expectation of being 'brilliant' can choose to avoid losing face by working ever harder. These are the ones who are likely to become obsessed with marks as a constant reaffirmation of their standing. Alternatively, they can decide to opt out, thereby avoiding situations where they might not do so well. This, in turn, can lead to a negative downward spiral of achievement: deteriorating working habits, excuses for not completing tasks, increasing dissatisfaction for the child and frustration for teachers and parents, and a lowering of the child's confidence and self-esteem.

If we see life as a continual process of exploration and experiment, we can learn as much, if not more, from our failures than we can from our successes. Therefore, while children need opportunities to experience success in order to gain in self-confidence, they also need opportunities to take risks, and even to fail, and to be encouraged to reflect on what they can learn from the 'failure'. We have to help children understand that only by having the courage to take risks will we ever discover our full capabilities. Just as gymnasts have to risk falling off the apparatus if they are to master complex sequences of movements, anyone who wants to improve their performance has to be willing to take risks, and accept the failures as part of their essential training.

So what can be done to help some young people relax their hold on a punishing and distorting self-image? We can:

- help children to develop a healthy, positive and realistic appreciation of themselves, and to establish good working habits, however difficult or easy they find it to learn;
- make sure we do not allow them from an early age to become locked into the trammels of unrelenting success;
- make sure that we provide learning situations where achievement is not measured only in traditional ways, but where the taking part, the effort given and the contribution that one makes to the learning of others are equally recognized and valued;
- base more of their learning on open-ended approaches that allow them to pursue their enquiries in a variety of ways;
- help them focus on their strategies for solving problems. Some very able children are disorganised in their approach to their work, having been able to reach solutions without giving much thought as to how they came to their conclusions. They may in fact be using faulty strategies, which can serve them well in the short term, but which will lead to difficulties when they meet more complex problems or issues to resolve. 'Detection, interpretation and remediation of one's errors is an important part of acquiring and making intelligent use of knowledge' (Wood 1999);
- provide resources and help them to learn strategies for regulating their own research and problem-solving, including having access to the world of learning through the use of information and communication technology. They will then be made constantly aware of how much more there is to know.

Labelling

'Being labelled gifted has distorted my life,' said Jeremy. This sentiment was echoed by Alison, another of the young people in Joan Freeman's study who is quoted as saying, 'Being labelled gifted has been the bane of my life' (Freeman 2001).

We use labels to help us organise our knowledge and ideas and to develop shared understandings with others. Labels are extremely useful. However, labels when linked to people can also be unhelpful and limit the way people think about one another. Labels can lead to people being categorised and to unwarranted assumptions being made about their attributes and likely behaviour. This is certainly a danger when it comes to thinking about children whose development is exceptional. A wise friend of mine used to urge: 'Label jars, not people'!

As we saw in Chapter 2, in Britain the term 'gifted' was widely used until well into the 1980s to describe children whose performance on standardised tests of intelligence placed them in the top 5 or 10 per cent of their age group. But many were unhappy with the term, believing it suggested that other children did not have 'gifts'. Terms such as 'very able' or 'highly able' became more widely used as these seemed to be less exclusive and restrictive. With the government's decision to reintroduce the term 'gifted' as part of the Excellence in Cities initiative and in all the DfES and OFSTED documents, we need to be aware of the potential implications for children and their families.

While the use of a descriptor can be useful as short-hand to help us talk about phenomena or events in a general way, it is unlikely to be helpful as a way of thinking about an individual. The term 'gifted' meaning 'ability to perform at a far higher level than expected' when used for a child can imply that this is an inherent characteristic, part of their individuality, a permanent condition such as eye colour. But children's development is never linear. Some may show precocious ability and talent at an early age but level off as they get older. Others may perform at a very high level in certain circumstances but not in others. And there are those whose interests and unusual skills only develop later in their lives. The label 'gifted' not only distorts the perception of an individual; it can also have an isolating and even alienating effect on their relationships. Parents, family members and school staff can be encouraged to have unrealistic expectations for the way the child will behave or continue to develop. For instance, in the Excellence in Cities initiative, what will happen when a child who has shown unusual ability or talent and been labelled 'gifted' in the primary school does not continue to shine later on? How will those children feel when having been led to believe their abilities and talents are outstanding they are later told they are not? How will this affect their parents and other family members? Is there not a danger that the child will fear that they are a disappointment and a failure? How too will it affect children who continue to perform at a very high level? Their self-concept as an unusual or gifted person will be strengthened even further.

Better by far to follow the same advice that is offered to parents and teachers when dealing with bad behaviour. Focus on the 'behaviour' and not on the child, otherwise the child learns to think of themselves as a bad person, rather than learning to identify what is bad about their behaviour. So with children who demonstrate exceptional abilities and talents it is possible to talk about those gifted or unusual behaviours that are evident at any one time, rather than the child as being gifted.

Acceleration

Children need opportunities to work with others in many contexts. They need to learn to appreciate the qualities and talents of children with a wide range of abilities. But they also need opportunities to work with others who can challenge and extend their thinking.

For children with exceptional ability, it will not always be easy to find a group of pupils with similar abilities with whom to work, especially where a child is working at a level that is three or more years above that of their classmates. Moving to an older class may provide an answer.

> **Mark**
>
> When Mark was only six years old his parents were keen for him to be moved into a class of eight-year-olds, as they believed his naughtiness at home stemmed from boredom and frustration at school. Sometimes moving the child into a higher class for all or for some of the time is thought to be the answer. This was indeed felt to be the case for Mark. He was already working on GCSE mathematics problems by the time he was eight, and had established himself very satisfactorily in a class of ten-year-olds. But such a provision had required special arrangements both within the school and with the school to which he was due to transfer.

Acceleration, or moving up into a class of older-aged children, can sometimes be used to solve the problem of being intellectually out of line from a peer group, but it has its complications. Such a move is almost always at the instigation of the parents and usually because they believe the child is bored or frustrated by working at the age-appropriate level and feel that this is having a damaging effect on their progress. There has been a lot of debate about the wisdom of such a solution to meeting a child's needs. Retrospective studies provide a mixed picture, with some people who had been accelerated reporting that they had continued to do well and had benefited from the arrangements. Others felt very differently and had not prospered. Their sense of alienation had increased by being put among children whose physical and social maturity was in advance of their own, especially as they moved into adolescence. By being entered early for public examinations they had not achieved the levels that they might have done had they taken them at the expected age (Montgomery 1996; Lee-Corbin and Denicolo 1998; Freeman 2001).

In coming to a decision about whether or not to accelerate a child, very careful thought must be given to their overall needs and welfare, as well as to the implications for the future. A short-term solution may create problems later when, for instance, the accelerated child may have to stay behind at the time of transfer to the secondary school, and friendship groups have to be disrupted. Children who have to repeat the final year in the primary school may find difficulties in making friends with children below their present class. They may feel distressed about losing their existing friends. They may lose interest and motivation and not want to cover similar work again. Alternatively, if the child moves up with the class of older children, difficulties may arise if the child finds that they are unable to fit in socially at a time when their peers move into interests and activities they are not ready to share. They may have difficulty in coping with the increasing demands of the next phase of schooling and they may not benefit in the longer term. There is no reliable evidence that acceleration results in higher performance at a later date.

Factors that must therefore be taken into account when looking at acceleration as a way of meeting a child's needs include:

- the child's birth date (whether they are among the oldest/youngest in the class)
- the child's overall level of maturity and whether the child can cope socially with an older age group
- whether the new class can provide a suitable learning environment
- how the receiving teacher feels about such a move
- how the child feels about the move
- how the parents feel
- the implication for transfer to the next school.

If possible, it is almost always preferable to find other alternatives that allow for flexibility in grouping for some aspects of the curriculum, but which do not rely on being moved into a class of older-aged children as the main solution.

Transition stages

Education is a continual process. It begins the day we are born, and continues to our life's end. However, within the formal educational system, there are several distinct phases: the preschool phase; the infant and junior, or primary years; secondary school and the wide range of further education opportunities. Such phases, or stages in education, are not necessarily based on predetermined patterns in children's development, nor are they the same even within or across Local Educational Authorities. Although the marking out of Key Stages in education has provided a structure for planning curriculum content, and monitoring children's progress and attainment, there is no common pattern to the organisation of schools in terms of the age range for which they provide. Thus a change of school and a move on to the 'next phase' can take place at almost any age dependent on the organisation of schools in any given area. While Key Stage 1 covers five- and six-year-olds, Key Stage 2 seven- to ten-year-olds, Key Stage 3 eleven- to fourteen-year-olds, and Key Stage 4 fifteen- and sixteen-year-olds, children can in fact transfer to a different school at the age of 5, 7, 8, 9, 11, 13, 14 or 16. Each arrangement has its merits and its disadvantages but all present new challenges for children.

Very bright children may experience a tension between their own growth patterns. Some bright all-rounders can develop physically earlier than most. They become much taller, stronger and more mature-looking than others in their class. Consequently, they may be treated as if they are in fact older and are then expected to behave with greater responsibility. The mismatch between such children and others can be felt acutely and become a source of embarrassment and distress. Some children may respond by trying to become as insignificant as possible, avoiding being marked out in any way. Unable to escape the distinguishing effects of size and physical maturity, they may attempt to avoid further attention by playing down their ability and deliberately reducing the quality of their work. Many very able children, previously excellent and enthusiastic students, disappoint their teachers during the later years in school. They are thought to be 'failing to live up to their promise'. Teachers may not realise that this is the child's attempt to fit in with the peer group. Some schools report that this is a bigger problem with boys than with girls. Other children may react differently. Some may assume leadership roles assigned to them because of their superior size and ability, but not necessarily in ways appreciated by the adult members of the community, or by other pupils.

Not all very bright children show this early growth spurt. Piaget, the noted child psychologist, proposed that between the ages of 9 and 13, significant physical and intellectual changes begin to take place. The onset of puberty not only marks the growth towards physical maturity; it is also linked to an intellectual growth, a significant widening of potential understanding and ability to deal with abstract concepts. For some children whose intellectual development is very precocious this move to adult ways of thinking can occur much earlier, even as young as seven. This may not be matched by a similar growth spurt or change in physical maturity. While beginning to think like adolescents, they remain child-sized. They may be unable to cope emotionally with the preoccupations of their minds. There may be a deeply distressing mismatch between their interests and those of their friends, between the kinds of things they want to discuss and the preoccupations of children of their own age. Longing to take part in adult discussions, to discuss the meaning of life, the concept of infinity, the idea of immortality, they may find that no-one is willing to share their concerns.

For these children the transition stages may be more than usually uncomfortable and induce feelings of intense frustration, loneliness, despair and even madness. When this happens children often seek relief by withdrawing into a private world of study, which only increases their sense of isolation. Or, as many parents recount, they look for contact with older children, sometimes imitating their ways in a desperate attempt to become accepted and perceived as more mature than they really are.

'A deep strangeness fell upon me, which made me feel all my life a sojourner on this planet rather than a native', wrote Norbert Weiner, who entered high school at the age of 10, alongside fellow students who were 17 years old. Weiner's case is highly unusual, but there are many children who find their unique pattern of development creates real difficulties, particularly at critical stages such as transition.

There are, however, huge age variations in the onset of puberty. As a general trend it is recognised that girls mature earlier than boys, but even within the sexes the differences are considerable. The growth spurt occurs in some children as early as 9 or 10 years, whereas in others it may not even be noticeable until they reach 15 or 16. Two factors in particular have implications for the way the transition stages in primary schools are managed. First, at no stage in their lives will the differences between children be so marked or so significant. Second, the onset of puberty is occurring earlier decade by decade. Whereas the problems of the adolescent stage used to be the concern of the secondary school, they are now reaching back and becoming part of the experience of the primary school as well. This has clear implications for the way educational provision is managed in that final year, if not earlier. For pupils with exceptional ability the problems may not be different in kind from those already described. But they are likely to differ in degree. Account must clearly be taken of the wide variations in pupils' development and their consequent need for appropriate levels of intellectual challenge and for personal support if they are not to feel alienated and demoralised at this critical stage in their education.

Pupils in their final years of primary school have usually lived within that educational community for a number of years. They have become familiar with the routines, the cycle of events, the expectations and demands within and outside the classroom. They have learned to adjust to the routines of the school and, in turn, to expect particular responses from their teachers. In fact, school may well have developed a predictability that some 10- and 11-year-olds begin to find tedious. During their last year they are encouraged to look forward to the new opportunities, the increased range of subjects, the more specialised equipment and resources, and the greater range of sporting facilities they will find in the next stage of education. At the same time, being 'senior members' of the school community, they are expected to accept additional responsibilities and remain committed to what is happening in their present school. This dual focus, with the need to achieve some balance at the centre of what must feel like a metaphorical 'seesaw', can result in some of the tensions that emerge at this stage.

Some children respond quite happily to the interests and demands of their special status. Others, particularly those who feel they have outgrown the primary school environment, may demonstrate their developing independence, strength and maturity in ways that their teachers find unhelpful, particularly if this entails a rejection of their authority.

James

James had always enjoyed school and had been a model student. He was recognised as being very bright, especially in mathematics and, until Year 6, he had worked hard and seemed happy to take part in class activities. Then there were signs of trouble. He became restless and demanding. He began to play around in class and challenge his teacher. She, in turn, became increasingly concerned and irritated by what she perceived to be a waste of the child's energies.

For the very bright, being in the top age group may represent an educational 'ceiling' previously avoided by the presence of older peers. A school may have organised its provision for the very able children with maximum flexibility and creativity, perhaps by allowing for alternative class arrangements or occasional groupings across different age ranges, or through clubs and other interest activities. Until children reach the final year they will always have had the potential opportunity of working with older children at some stage, or mixing with them informally and thereby enjoying the stimulus of intellectual compatibility. However, once they reach the last year, there will be no older children on hand with whom to share such experiences. Opportunities for growth through sharing and exploring directly with other children will therefore be restricted to those available within the existing class or classes in the school, and these may be insufficient.

Furthermore, a very bright child's level of functioning in a subject may have progressed beyond the competence and confidence of the teacher, particularly in such subjects as mathematics and science. The teacher may be hard put to know how to present interesting and challenging problems that match the very bright child's ability. When James's parents were invited into school to discuss the deterioration in his behaviour, his teacher learned that he had done a GCSE mathematics paper at home for fun, and was reading technical books on astronomy. This would not be an uncommon experience for such children. A study of the issues facing teachers of Year 6 pupils, carried out in a number of Oxfordshire primary schools, reported that many teachers find it difficult to challenge very able pupils in areas of the curriculum where they are not subject specialists (Eyre and Fuller 1993). The problem is especially acute in small schools where teachers have to take responsibility for a number of different subjects, and where there may be less opportunity to develop the knowledge and expertise to teach very bright children.

As we have seen in the section on pages 43–4 on acceleration, schools and parents sometimes try to solve the problem by arranging an early transfer to the secondary school. The advantage of this is that the children may receive the stimulus and intellectual challenges suited to their ability, and they are able to study a wider range of subjects. In a recent study it was found that early transfer to secondary school was beneficial for some children, especially those from small rural schools (Hymer, B. and Harbron, N., in Lee-Corbin and Denicolo 1998). However, this is by no means a universal solution. For one thing, many exceptional children are not one, but two, three or even more years ahead of their contemporaries. For another, exceptional ability does not always generalise to all aspects of learning, nor, as already discussed, is it necessarily matched by a similar emotional maturity. The interests and feelings of a child who has not yet begun the puberty phase are very different from that of the adolescent. By being placed in a group of older children, very bright younger children may find themselves in a social grouping with which they are unable to cope. The pros and cons of acceleration at 'transition stages' are discussed further on page 44.

There are no simple solutions, nor a single blueprint for managing these situations. But clusters of schools have developed a number of joint strategies to meet particular circumstances and the needs of specific pupils. For instance, cooperation between a family of feeder schools might result in the pooling of talent, expertise and interests of the teachers in order to provide extension studies. These and other approaches will be discussed in Chapter 9, on school organisation and provision.

Family relationships

In Chapters 3 and 4, on early development, we considered the impact of the widening of the exceptional child's experience beyond the family and the home. We also need to consider the possible implications within the family itself.

An unusually bright or talented child is likely to absorb a disproportionate share of the family's attention. This is also often the case where a child has other individual needs that call for a great deal of care and support. In such circumstances there is always a danger that the needs of other members of the family are overlooked. It is easy to slip into a pattern whereby one child becomes the main focus of the adults' attention and their needs always come first. Where the focus of parental interest is centred on one child whom they have identified as exceptional, the talents of the other equally able siblings can sometimes be undervalued. If one child's development appears precocious, or unusual talents and abilities begin to emerge, the family may need to take a serious look at the way the family interest is being shared. If it becomes unbalanced with one member becoming the centre of attention, there may be unhelpful consequences. The precocious child may be encouraged to develop an unrealistic sense of their own importance. This may result in the child devaluing the rights of other siblings and to think disparagingly of others. The focus child also risks becoming an object of envy and dislike. Brothers and sisters who feel neglected may come to feel jealous and rejecting of the child they see as taking all their parents' attention.

The family is the first community the child meets and one of its central functions at this stage is to help children discover how important other people are. So, it is essential that the early experience within the family encourages a child to learn to respect others, to cooperate, to wait their turn and sometimes to modify their own demands for the sake of a common need. Parents who do not provide such teaching instead are not serving their children, who may find great difficulty in establishing happy relationships in groups outside the home.

As parents it is natural to take pride in our children's achievements. We all want them to do well, and to lead interesting and productive lives. But we must guard against investing too much of ourselves in our expectations for their future, of burdening them with our own 'dreams'. Children can sometimes provide for their parents the success or the public esteem that has been lacking in their parents' own lives. They can sometimes compensate for past disappointments and opportunities missed. This is a very real risk for children who show unusual talent or ability.

Marie

Marie was a promising musician. She started piano lessons at the age of 5, and was soon the star soloist in school concerts. Her mother had also been a talented performer, but had not been able to pursue her career in music due to family difficulties. She was delighted by the emergence of her daughter's gifts and devoted a great deal of time, energy and money to supporting Maria's musical development. When later, as a teenager, the girl no longer wished to spend long hours practising and became increasingly reluctant to carry on with her piano lessons, her mother was intensely disappointed.

When too much emphasis is laid on success and results children may feel compelled to achieve and thereby become harnessed to the shackles of success. They may grow to believe that they must do well to retain the love and affection of their parents. Failure to be outstanding then truly becomes something to be feared. We need to be sure that we understand the difference between the pleasure and pride we feel for the *child,* and the pleasure and pride we take for *ourselves.* The first will support the child; the second can be an unwelcome burden.

Parents may have to work hard to identify which activities belong to them, and which belong to the children. This becomes particularly important when it concerns the activities which involve them as a *family.* Joining a 'club' for clever or talented children is especially liable to provoke such situations as Michael's.

Michael

It was clear from an early age that Michael was very bright. He was constantly on the move, developing passionate and sometimes obsessive interests. He read voraciously and spent long hours in his room working on his computer. He sometimes complained that he had no-one with whom to share his interests. Michael's parents were both pleased and proud that their son was showing such a level of intellectual ability, but they were also somewhat bemused. They joined a local organisation that ran sessions on a Saturday for very able children, and greatly enjoyed the social opportunities and moral support this offered them. When Michael lost interest in attending, his parents initially felt deprived of an important focus in their lives. Later, once they had been able to sort out the difference between what Michael wanted and what they needed for themselves, they decided to continue to attend the sessions as volunteer helpers.

Of course, for many children, organisations such as the National Association for Gifted Children (NAGC) or the centre for Children of High Intelligence (CHI) provide a lifeline, a real source of support for them and their families. They give children an opportunity to meet with others who share similar interests and to take part in a range of stimulating and challenging activities. They also provide parents with much-valued opportunities to talk to others who understand the issues of living with an unusually bright child. However, there is a risk that the very act of joining an organisation so firmly linked to 'giftedness' will encourage the family to increase even further the emphasis they put on the child's ability or talent. Parents may come to depend too heavily on the benefits for themselves in belonging to the group. They might thereby be unwittingly putting further pressure on their child to continue to show interest in attending the sessions or to continue to demonstrate 'gifted' behaviour. Where parents are aware of the risks and are able to keep a focus on meeting their child's needs in as many and varied ways as possible, the support from special interest organisations can be invaluable. The challenge for parents is to see their children as unique individuals with a development and personality all of their own, and to have the courage and sensitivity to balance the need to provide encouragement with a restraint of personal needs to distort the natural inclinations and pursuits of the child.

CHAPTER 6

Adolescence

Conflicting demands

In Britain, we have a culture that does not always value academic success. Ask anyone what their mental image of a very clever child looks like, and likely as not they will come up with a version of a 'nerd' or a boffin, a poor physical specimen, with heavy glasses and eyes weakened through excessive study, and spindly limbs due to lack of healthy exercise. Throughout the country we have a very real problem of underachievement, particularly among boys. In far too many schools it is not 'cool' to be clever. Take this description from one boy's science teacher:

Martin

Martin is a walking disaster. He seems to live in a world of his own. He is never where he should be. If he ever does turn up to the right lesson he is invariably late. He really doesn't seem to know whether he's coming or going. As for his work, it is quite disgraceful. He is extremely reluctant to put anything down on paper, and quite honestly, when he does it's so untidy, so carelessly done that I quite often refuse to mark it. And yet . . . and yet there's something about the lad that makes me wonder. When he does get interested in what we're doing he asks the most extraordinary questions. Really intelligent and perceptive ones. He often seems to see the solution to a problem before others have even understood the question and he enjoys looking for alternative ways of reaching a conclusion. In fact, when he stops playing the class clown he can be really quite profound.

Then there was Joanna:

Joanna

She's a model pupil. Her work is quite outstanding. Her particular interest seems to be in history, but she is without doubt the most able mathematician in her year, and she is going to be something of a linguist too. She's such a pleasure to have in the class. She's very popular, of course; she's so mature, a born leader.

There is no guarantee that the potential shown by children in the primary years will continue and develop throughout their school career. Excellence in performance requires not only talent and ability but also commitment, determination and a willingness to put in enormous amounts of effort. It is also to do with the ethos of the school and its attitudes to learning, sport, culture and the community. It is somehow easier to accept the truth of this assertion when we consider that it takes talent plus exceptional hard work and practice, as well as support, to become an outstanding athlete, musician or dancer. We tend not to think the same holds true for performing at the highest academic level. It is as if we want to think that if we are 'clever', success will always come easily. But this is very rarely the case. No-one reaches the top of their chosen field simply by having talent. Studies of people who have become outstanding performers almost invariably show that the common factor in all their lives has been a high degree of motivation, an ability to dedicate themselves to reaching a goal, a willingness to put in hours and hours of sheer hard work, and support from their families (Freeman *et al.* 1995; Howe 1996). To achieve at a very high level is rather like baking a cake: you need the basic ingredients of above-average ability, high motivation and favourable circumstances.

The problem is that for young people in our western society, learning and study requirements become more onerous and demanding at the very time in their personal development when they have other more interesting and important preoccupations. They are entering the stage of their lives we call adolescence.

Adolescence is a time in young people's lives that can be fraught with tensions, emotions and anxieties. It is a period when a young person has to move on and outwards from the child who they were, defined in part by their parents and their environment, to become a person created in their own terms. This exciting but troubling process of discovering and defining a new self involves a drawing away from one's parents and other familiar adults, a growing acceptance of a new physical self, and the management of powerful and troubling emotions. A useful way of understanding what happens during this 'transformation' phase of life has been put forward by the psychologist W. D. Wall. He wrote about the young person embarking on the task of constructing four distinct but intricately related selves: a sexual self, a social self, a vocational self and a philosophical/moral self (Wall 1968). The development of these various aspects of themselves in order to build a new and separate adult identity will inevitably involve young people in an extended period of experimentation, readjustment and growth, both within themselves and in the context of their relationships with others.

First, there are quite obvious and quite unavoidable physiological developments: the body expands, upwards and outwards, often at a sudden and alarming rate, facial features become transformed, body shape alters, hair appears on previously smooth parts of the anatomy, bulges emerge, skin takes on a different quality and texture. These changes, accompanied as they are by hormonal developments affecting sensation and mood, are simultaneously intensely fascinating and a source of anxiety and apprehension. Imagine how we would feel as adults if a similar reshaping of our features and body structure were suddenly to take place. In the normal course of events these body changes and developments begin at around the time that significant intellectual growth occurs. Young people's ability to view events only from their own perspective, to consider the world only in relation to their own experience, expands into an ability to transcend their own immediate thoughts and to consider many possible points of view. Two significant things follow as a result: young people become able to turn their eyes upon themselves, from the outside, as it were, seeing themselves as others might see them; and they become capable of thinking about the nature of thought, of holding a number of possible hypotheses at once and reasoning between them. They learn to 'play' with ideas. The initial experiences are understandably both exciting and alarming. Being able to turn one's own eyes upon oneself carries with it the discomfort of seeing, or imagining, the blemishes as well as the beauties. Finding that one's body is behaving in such unpredictable, and not always welcome, ways can cause embarrassment and anxiety. This also confronts the young person with the pain of acknowledging the gap that exists between what is the reality and what is the dream.

Figure 6.1 The pain of acknowledging the gap between the reality and the dream

Much of the adolescent obsession with the narcissistic reflection in the mirror and excessive self-criticism is based on the need to adjust to the new emerging self, and to come to terms with what is happening. It is also to do with the fact that this is an intermediary period, where the differentiation of oneself from others, of one's thoughts from the opinions of others', is not fully accomplished. It is a period of great imbalance. Young people, able to see themselves from the outside and to reflect upon their own thoughts, find themselves fascinating and imagine everyone else must do so too. Everything they admire about themselves must be admired by others; any perceived blemish must be equally despised. The disparities between the realities of the present and their dreams for the future may result in feelings of resentment towards a world which is so obviously determined to thwart the realisation of their ideals.

The new-found ability to juggle with ideas encourages a state of indecisiveness that often infuriates adults, and drives young people to seek support from their peers. It is the time of peer group bonding, of 'us against the world', where the approval of one's friends is far more important than that of adults. Together they can complain about the ignorance of the adult world, and construct their own imaginary El Dorado. All things become possible because solutions can always be found in the endlessly creative mind.

For young people whose development is out of line with their peers', or who cannot find a peer group to which they feel they belong, this can be a time of great stress. Their ability to look critically at the world and the people within it, and to weigh up the differences between the 'actual' and the 'ideal', may far outstrip their emotional ability to cope with their new ways of thinking. While many children with exceptional ability do achieve a happy balance between their intellectual and social development, some do not.

Martin and Joanna provide striking examples. The problems they were facing were not unique or particularly unusual. To a great extent they were similar to problems faced by all young persons at some stage of their development. The only difference between their experience and that of others seemed to be one of intensity, and of timing.

Martin

Martin had begun to ponder on questions of world significance while still at junior school. He had found himself growing increasingly aware of his parents' and his teachers' failings, and angry with what he felt to be gaps in their understanding. While still a child, his intellectual development had leapt ahead, leaving him emotionally bewildered and unhappy. No compensatory physiological changes were taking place at that time to divert his attention. No-one else around seemed to share his experience. He felt truly alone. He wanted to shut his mental eyes and return to the happier unquestioning state he still remembered, but he could not. His thoughts would not allow him to do so. So began for him the bad period, when he became restless and confused within himself and a puzzle to his family and friends. Later, when he did begin to develop physically, the whole process became unbearable to him. His body betrayed him. It grew large and ugly. His arms and legs developed a life of their own. Martin looked a mess and he hated himself. Gone were the cherished thoughts of himself as the fictional hero. What he saw in the mirror was a travesty of the brilliance of the inner person.

Furthermore, Martin was experiencing great difficulty with the early stages of reading and writing. As a result he was not only frustrated by the betrayal of his physical appearance, but was also intellectually trapped, unable to give proper expression to his thinking in the ways that were valued in school. He looked a mess. His work looked a mess. He disowned himself. He became a clown. Martin had given up on the world of adults. In his eyes, no-one outside himself was of any worth. No-one, he believed, was able to understand him, share in his interests or recognise the brilliance and uniqueness of his thoughts. Teachers especially were worthy only of his contempt. Teachers, he said, clearly cared nothing for the real life of their pupils; they had never taken the trouble to get to know *him*. They had always treated him as though he were stupid, whereas it was they, in fact, who were ignorant. Most of the time they would not let him ask questions or express his views because they realised they could not cope with what he wanted to discuss. He knew they had to keep their distance and behave like robots just to keep control. Bitter, disillusioned, Martin was only 13 years old.

Joanna

Joanna faced a different kind of problem. She had matured both physically and intellectually at an even pace, but was way ahead of her classmates. The elder daughter in a family of two, her parents both teachers, she basked in their loving support. Her father's passionate interest in history soon became her own. Together they visited museums and took part in archaeological digs at weekends. Her mother had a background in modern languages and the family spoke French at meal times. Joanna had always been a loving, sociable child: a source of pride and delight to her parents; a much prized pupil to all her teachers. She had been recognised as being exceptionally bright from a very early age and had been encouraged throughout her school career. Joanna was destined for high academic and social success. Unlike Martin, Joanna believed in the fundamental integrity of teachers. She too could recognise human failings and the need to keep face at times of challenge. But Joanna empathised with her teachers. She said she understood the difficulties. She, like Martin, was often despairingly bored. 'But,' she said, 'it's often my fault. I always read ahead so of course I get bored if we have to go over it all again in class. It must be very difficult for a teacher to have someone in the class like me. After all, they have to help all those who take longer to understand. That's only fair.'

Joanna was also only just 13. In many ways she was mature beyond her years. To many, Joanna did not seem to have a problem. But as we discussed her work it became clear that it was fear of adult disapproval that was preventing her from expressing her real feelings of frustration. She had a natural empathy and sensitivity towards the feelings of others and a precocious ability to identify with their experience. She also needed to be thought of as a 'good' girl, a 'good' student, which encouraged her compliancy. Joanna, like Martin, was not well understood by her teachers. The difficulty for Joanna, as she moved into adolescence, would be in exploring her true self, developing her independent opinions and establishing her own identity.

No two youngsters could have been more contrasting than were Martin and Joanna. Yet they shared common dilemmas that invariably face all young people. They also both experienced a particular confusion in experiencing an adolescence that was precocious and, in Martin's case, unequally balanced. As such it presented them with a personal challenge that was indeed rather special. Their particular paths to maturity were made easier once the adults involved began to recognise the problems, and were willing to help the youngsters develop their special talents more constructively and in ways that reflected their unique identity. This is not always an easy task as it can make heavy demands on one's patience and ingenuity. It demands personal maturity and courage to look at relationships with young people with honesty. It means recognising that very bright youngsters may be just as much in need of guidance and personal support as others with more evident difficulties. It certainly requires a thorough examination of the opportunities offered to youngsters within a school's organisation.

The issue of gender

'I well remember making a conscious decision about this when I was 14,' said Jenny. We were talking about the difficulties many girls experience in trying to reconcile the fact of being clever *and* feminine. 'It felt like a choice at the time. I sensed it would have to be either one or the other, that I could not, or would certainly not, be accepted as being able to be both. Of course I think things have changed now, but I believe a lot of the old prejudices and stereotyping are still around.'

And indeed they are. We have already seen that there are pressures during a child's early life and school career to persuade them to conform to expectations and, in the case of clever children, to dissuade them from making their exceptional abilities too obvious. Once children reach secondary age, the pressures may continue to be affected by gender expectations. Gender expectation affects both boys and girls and in different ways.

A number of research studies have produced evidence that suggests that there are different patterns of neurological development between boy and girl babies which predispose them to different early development of particular skills and interests. Such studies have also shown that boys and girls may have different rates and types of intellectual (as well as physical) development and that these may have a bearing on their response to and performance in particular subjects. For instance little boys seem to be more interested in play that involves making, doing and exploring the properties of objects which might lead to a greater propensity for, and interest in, the practical aspects of mathematics and science. The greater interest for many little girls in talking and cooperative and social play may lead to their greater advantage in language-based activities (Fox and Zimmerman 1985; Walden and Walkerdine 1985; Freeman 1991).

Whatever the neurophysiological facts about brain development, the belief that the 'capacity' of the female brain is different from that of the male, is unhelpful when it comes to children's development and relationships, as misinterpretation can lead to the information being used in inappropriate ways. This can lead to generalisations which distort people's views of one another and deny the uniqueness of the individual. It is more important to be aware of those factors that influence the way children develop, and make sure that as adults we do nothing that puts limits on children's expectations. If children are allowed to think they are not capable of doing something well they are likely to develop this as a personal 'belief', and to become trapped within the limitations of an unhealthy 'can't do' mythology: 'I'm no good at maths, drawing, games, singing…'. The reality may be that they have never been encouraged to work at and improve the skill.

There are a number of different pressures on girls and boys, particularly in adolescence. They tend to be based on cultural factors and what we deem to be expected 'male' or 'female' qualities and behaviour. Sometimes, qualities which when attributed to men are described as strong-mindedness, decisiveness and the ability to persevere are interpreted as domineering, ruthless or obstinate when attributed to women. As a result some girls deliberately choose to subdue their responses to conform to social expectations. Vanessa, for instance, had earned something of a reputation in her class. She had a sharp wit and an ability to go straight to the point. In class discussions she would express her views clearly and concisely, often having effectively dismissed the arguments put by others. She was aware she was thought to be bossy and a know-all. 'Fat chance she has of getting a boyfriend,' said fellow students. Carol, on the other hand, chose not to take an active part in class debates. She had to be encouraged to volunteer an opinion. When she did, she measured her words carefully, and tried not to say anything too controversial. Yet beneath her compliant facade Carol was just as aware as Vanessa about the issues and the lack of substance or logic in the arguments presented by her companions. But she preferred to be 'one of the group'. For Carol, the desire for social success resulted in the denial of her intellectual self. She, like Jenny, had made a choice between being popular, conforming to expectations of her gender and being clever.

Boys too may be subjected to a number of pressures. While expectations of the role of men have changed significantly in recent years there are still a number of prejudices around, particularly among adolescents. Boys may be mocked if their particular interest or talent does not conform to the still popular stereotypes of appropriate 'male' behaviour. We still associate sensitivity and the open expression of feelings with femininity. We encourage this in girls, but in the past we tended to discourage it in boys. The notion of 'Big boys don't cry' is still around in many families. A sensitive boy, with real

Figure 6.2 A choice between being popular and being clever

insight into creative experience, who wants to dance or write poetry, who responds with emotion to artistic expression, may well have a hard time in many of our schools. His talents and imagination can be crushed and driven out through mockery. The desire to create an acceptable masculine image for himself can force a choice on a boy as unfortunate and as unnecessary as the one that can face girls. Boys may well be discouraged from following certain courses because to do so would expose them to the embarrassment of being the only boy among a class of girls, or to the mocking remarks of peers.

We also need to take note of research that shows that from earliest childhood families tend to encourage boys more than girls to become independent, self-reliant and able to assume responsibility, the very qualities that underpin high performance (Fox and Zimmerman 1985; Freeman 1996). Differences in early encouragement of such qualities almost certainly affect the behaviour and achievements of boys and girls in school. Such family and cultural influences may also lie behind evidence of other differences in children's responses to their work. In a number of studies boys have been shown to be more ready to see their successes as due to their ability, whereas girls tend more often to attribute their success to good luck or the fact that they worked hard, or the task was easy. Boys are more likely to attribute failure at a task to their lack of effort, whereas girls are more likely to attribute it to a lack of ability (Deaux and Emswiller 1974; Freeman 1991a). Girls may also be reluctant to attribute success to their ability for fear of seeming to brag, this being considered an unattractive trait in girls (Heatherington *et al.* 1989). Teachers may also unwittingly reinforce these misguided gender stereotypes. Various research studies have shown how some teachers use praise differently

depending on whether the pupil is a boy or a girl. In these studies, teachers were more likely to praise a boy for doing well in a subject, attributing his success to his ability, and to reprimand his 'lack of effort' if he did not do well. Girls, on the other hand, were more likely to be praised for having made an effort when they achieved success, and their failures were considered to result from a lack of understanding or skill rather than poor effort (Dweck *et al.* in Wood 1999). If we become more aware of the ways that social factors and our own behaviour affect young people's response to their work, we can take steps to avoid some of the problems before they arise.

Fortunately, there has been a dramatic change in recent years. In fact, we have reached a situation where girls now regularly outperform boys in almost all areas of the curriculum. By the year 2000 girls were outperforming boys in all public examinations at school in all subjects other than physics. Also, in 2001, for the first time, women gained more first class degrees than men (Freeman 2001). For many schools the challenge now is to overcome a culture of underachievement among boys, which is just as damaging as the one which used to limit the expectations of girls.

But in some families and communities the old prejudices and stereotypic attitudes remain and can diminish expectations and aspirations of young people. We must continue to watch for those influences that deter any young person from pursuing paths which are best suited to their talents. Schools can review their own practice and examine their policies to see what they are currently doing, or what they could do, to encourage children's confidence and self-belief. Parents and teachers can examine their own attitudes and behaviour to see whether they are encouraging conformity in girls but accepting more aggressive and exploratory behaviour in boys. They can help dispel the myth that if you make use of your ability to the full you will be unattractive, and actively encourage girls as well as boys to challenge and to be constructively assertive. After all, adults can be the role models for the attitudes and values they want to promote. They can regularly and openly discuss the subject of gender roles and stereotyping, and encourage young people to explore their feelings and expectations. They can set high expectations for all children and refuse to be satisfied with anything but the best from each individual. Teachers can provide frequent positive feedback which goes beyond the high marks that very able pupils often obtain. Schools can also encourage pupils to take part in out of school activities that introduce them to interests that they may not have previously considered appropriate for their gender. They can enlist the help of parents to make sure that they too play their part in encouraging their children to be bold and true to themselves and to value their individuality.

PART 2

Providing for More Able Pupils

CHAPTER 7

Meeting the needs of more able pupils

Education is not the filling of a pail but the lighting of a fire.

W. B. Yeats

It has long been recognised that in Britain, at least, the needs of more able children or those with exceptional abilities and talents have been largely overlooked. Many national surveys and official reports have commented on the general lack of attention given to these children's particular educational entitlements (HMI 1979, 1985, 1992; DES 1989).

In 1999 a House of Commons Select Committee report *Highly Able Children* stated that many able children were being let down by the school system and as a result they were not achieving as well as they might. Following extensive consultation the committee concluded that, in too many schools, expectations were not sufficiently high and the ethos did not support a drive for high academic or intellectual achievement. Many teachers were thought to be unsure about the most effective ways of recognising high potential or about provision for appropriate learning experiences for highly able children. Underachievement was therefore resulting in a lamentable waste of talent and a potential loss for the country. The Select Committee also concluded that there was no single 'best' way to meet these children's needs and that the emphasis must be on improving provision in mainstream schools. This, they felt, would raise standards of attainment for all pupils (Education and Employment Committee 1999).

Since that time the education of highly able pupils has achieved a much higher profile. An Advisory Committee was formed to advise the government on the needs of the children and on policies that would improve practice in schools. In March 1999 the government launched the 'Excellence in Cities' initiative in which one of the main 'strands' concerned the development of provision for the most able pupils. Piloted first in secondary schools in Local Authorities taking part in the project, the Gifted and Talented project has since expanded to a wider group of Local Authorities and into primary schools. A key aim is to develop strategies for organising and extending the curriculum and for managing provision across clusters of schools. These are expected to provide useful models for other schools to consider.

In order to support schools and teachers further in their work with able pupils the Department for Education and Employment (DfEE) and the Qualifications and Curriculum Authority (QCA) have been producing a range of documents and written guidance (*National Literacy and Numeracy Strategies: Guidance on teaching able children*, 2000; *Guidance on Teaching Gifted and Talented Pupils*, 2001). The progress of highly able pupils is now also closely monitored through the national inspection arrangements. The Office for Standards in Education (OFSTED) handbook and *Evaluating Educational Inclusion* set out the requirements on inspectors for inspecting and evaluating the progress and attainment of very able pupils and the provision that is being made to meet their needs. There are also plans to ensure that an introduction to the teaching of 'Gifted and Talented' pupils is included in all initial teacher training courses.

The situation is therefore now very different from the time when parents of children with exceptional ability were not sure how they should expect their local school to respond to their concerns about provision. But it takes time for developments to take place, and teachers have to be given encouragement and support to develop their own understandings and skills. The following chapters are concerned with the main issues concerning provision in schools. They provide a 'starting point' for schools and teachers who may then be encouraged to develop their practice further, making use of the many excellent and more detailed publications that are now available (see Reference sections).

CHAPTER 8

Recognising and assessing abilities

Ways and means

Being able to recognise and assess high ability in children is not about 'talent spotting' as an end in itself. The purpose of recognising and assessing children's abilities is to determine what children know, understand and can already do, in order to plan appropriate learning opportunities. It is important for all children, whatever the level of their ability, that teachers understand the way they learn and have a good idea about what they are capable of doing. If teachers are to be able to provide for all children in their classes, they need to be alert to those pupils for whom more challenging work is appropriate.

We also need to be sure that we are providing children with opportunities to *demonstrate* the knowledge, skills and understandings in which we are interested. Children will only be able to demonstrate their talents if they are provided with the opportunities and means to do so. No child became an accomplished violinist without being given a violin or became an athlete without the chance to practise. For instance, Stephen Hawking might not have been able to demonstrate his theories about the universe had he lived in a different age and not been given access to the technology that has allowed him to share his knowledge with the world. The opportunities provided for children to explore their talents also need to take account of the multi-dimensional nature of human intelligence and performance, enabling them to exercise the full range of qualities and characteristics set out in Gardner's model of multiple intelligences (Gardner 1990).

Children are unique individuals and their responses to learning experiences will vary. As we have seen in previous chapters, some may have no difficulty in demonstrating their talents and abilities through the quality of their performance and through their ability to communicate their knowledge. Others may not. For instance, there is no difficulty in recognising that Ruth, in her poem *Metamorphosis of Narcissus*, is demonstrating an unusual gift for language and imagination for a child her age.

Metamorphosis of Narcissus
(Poem based on Salvador Dali painting, by Ruth Larbey, aged 10)

Nimbus clouds whisping about in a great turmoil of action.
A pond with no movement breaking the thin film-like surface.
The sun rising above the jagged mountains in the far distance
in a land where all things mythical and real live together in perfect harmony
In a land where the sun and moon come together to paint the sky the most amazing
colours and hues.
Now, in a world of change, a great feat.
The great god Narcissus is stirred to finally waken from his deep slumber.
Out of the pond and into the wide world, metamorphosis takes place,
and into man form he changes,
And there in the cave of fantasy he dwells ad infinitum.

In the primary phase of education, systems for recognising and assessing children's abilities may rely heavily on the professional opinion of one class teacher, supplemented by information from tests and other sources. In the secondary phase, where a child will be known by many teachers, the process will be more about sharing information about the child's responses to different settings and to different subjects. However, it can be more difficult to recognise the potential abilities and talents of children who are underachieving. Schools need to make sure that they are not only acknowledging the talents of those who are already high attainers; they also need to ensure that they are using all the available information and that they are taking account of factors that affect performance, such as motivation, personality, home background and any special difficulties. If we want to be sure that we remain alert to all the evidence that is available we need to adopt an eclectic approach, recognising that any one approach will have its limitations. A comprehensive approach would include the following evidence:

Parental information
Parents and other people who have responsibility for the care of children are an under-used source of valuable information. They have access to the most detailed and intimate knowledge about their child and their information can provide additional insight on their child's needs. They can provide useful information on their child's interests and hobbies, the clubs they attend or their sporting activities. Some schools ask prospective parents about these wider aspects of the child's life, as part their regular information gathering on entry to school.

Teacher nomination

Class or subject teachers are likely to be in the best position to recognise a child's ability. They will know, from their experience in teaching many children, what is generally expected of children of different ages and what seems to be unusual in terms of quality or the level of skill.

However, research suggests that teachers can underestimate what a child can do (Gottfried *et al.* 1994). Sometimes too much emphasis is placed on the child producing neat work and creativity is misunderstood or undervalued. Children's behaviour can also affect how teachers think about a child's abilities. For example, children are more likely to be considered able if they read early, speak confidently, use sophisticated vocabulary, demonstrate a good general knowledge, are lively and attentive, present their work neatly, perform at a high level of skill and behave in a mature manner. However, equally able children may be overlooked if they are quiet or withdrawn, slow to develop reading and writing skills, produce untidy work, have limited outside school experiences, use English as a second language, have additional special educational needs or are badly behaved.

Where teacher nomination is used it is important to track the child's performance across all subjects. Subject teachers also need to agree on what they consider constitutes high-level performance in their particular area of learning.

Checklists

Checklists of the characteristics of high ability can sometimes be useful as 'pointers'. They are reminders of some of the clues that we can look for and which can lead us to ask further questions about how the child is learning. They can also help avoid the risk of overlooking pupils' potential ability when a child may not be producing written work of a high quality. Able and talented children may think and learn easily and quickly, display extensive general knowledge, and show advanced understanding for their age and an ability to communicate their many and varied ideas. They may show great curiosity, ask challenging questions and demonstrate an ability to relate new ideas to previous knowledge and experiences. They also may have a vivid imagination. Some may have a distinctive sense of humour and enjoy playing around with language and ideas. Quite often they show they can concentrate for long periods of a time, even when quite young, and develop very strong interests. However, a highly able child may show none of these characteristics, so it is important to treat checklists with caution. An example of a checklist is provided in the Appendix.

Subject specific checklists that are based on what has been agreed to be features of high-level performance in a subject area are much more useful, especially at the secondary school level. These not only provide an indication of what children could demonstrate in their learning, but they can also serve as the basis for planning learning experiences, and teaching strategies that call upon high-level thinking and response. The QCA guidance for teaching gifted and talented pupils provides a very useful framework (QCA 2001).

School records

School records can provide useful information on what children can already do and may give clues as to whether their progress and development is in any way unusual. Entry Profile data, Baseline Assessment tests and other information gathered at the time of admission to a new school will all provide valuable information about how children are developing and learning. Such information is particularly helpful if it includes the evidence of parents. School records can also shed light on children's development over time, alerting teachers to a possible change in motivation and expected progress, perhaps as a response to personal circumstances or school arrangements.

Tests

Standardised tests

Standardised tests are designed to compare a person's performance with that of others of a similar age. Individual or group tests usually produce a standardised score or percentile ranking which allows the identification of those people who perform at a lower or higher level than expected for that age group, or within the expected range.

Some intelligence tests assess 'general' reasoning ability. The individually administered Wechsler Intelligence Scale (WISC) and the British Ability Scales (BAS) are examples of these. While the WISC and the BAS both produce a 'global' IQ score, they also permit examination and comparisons between the test subscales that contribute to the global score. The main limitations regarding the use of these tests are the costly training requirements for those who administer them, the fact that they can only be used individually and the time taken in their administration. However, there are other tests such as those produced by NFER, which are standardised on the British population and which can be used with groups as well as whole classes of children. These include tests that assess verbal, numerical and non-verbal reasoning. More recently, many schools have introduced the 'Cognitive Ability Tests' which also provide standardised scores for a range of thinking and reasoning abilities.

In the case of highly able children all these tests can be useful in highlighting pupils who score at the top end of the percentile ranking. For instance, a score of 130 places a child among the top 10 per cent of children doing the same test. A score of 140 places them in the top 1 per cent. Such information from these tests may prove useful where there is any discrepancy between the children's potential as measured by the tests and their actual performance in school. Where such a discrepancy does exist, questions can be raised as to what might be happening to limit the children's achievements.

However, the results of any test must be treated with caution. Test reliability and validity are always subject to factors such as weakness in test construction, children's willingness to respond on the day, cultural bias and differences in the way in which the tests were carried out by the teachers. Tests can also only provide information on those aspects of human ability and performance they are designed to assess. The information provided by a global IQ score is particularly limited and highly influenced by the theory of intelligence held by the persons who constructed the tests and the items that they chose to include within them. 'An intelligence quotient may be of provisional value as a first crude approximation when the mental level of an individual is sought,' said the psychologist William Stern, writing in 1938, 'but whoever imagines that in determining this quality he has summed up the intelligence of an individual once and for all, leaves off where psychology should begin.'

Criterion-referenced tests
Criterion-referenced tests are tests that assess performance against set criteria: whether a child can do what we ask them to do. Children can be asked to demonstrate that they can spell a given set of words, perform certain mathematical calculations, follow a set of instructions, give a correct answer to a problem. Standard Assessment Tasks (SATs) at the end of Key Stages 1, 2 and 3 are examples of criterion-referenced tests. Some GCSE examinations and the General National Vocational Qualifications (GNVQ) are also criterion-referenced. Such tests are useful in providing information on what a child or young person knows, understands and can do in a given curriculum area or skill. But, as the criteria are set in advance, the results do not necessarily show what the child might be capable of doing and what else they could achieve. The tests are also very likely to be influenced by the quality of teaching the child has received.

Assessment through the curriculum
One of the most effective ways of recognising children's abilities is by providing them with a wide range of learning opportunities through which they can demonstrate their understanding and skills. But, as was stated at the beginning of this chapter, children will only be able to demonstrate their talents if they have the means to do so. You will never know how high a child can jump unless you keep raising the bar. You will never be able to explore the extent of children's ability to think without giving them the chance to stretch their thinking muscles, to respond to increasingly challenging questions in

their everyday work in the classroom. Children's work may show you quite clearly how they are thinking and whether this is evidence of anything unusual.

Figure 8.1 Matthew, aged 6, introducing movement and perspective into his drawings

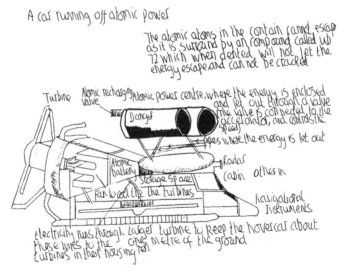

Figure 8.2 Kevin, aged 11

Information from children

Discussions with children can provide important information on their interests and the activities in which they take part outside the school. These may indicate abilities and talents that may not otherwise be apparent. This may be especially useful where a child is not showing interest for general schoolwork but nevertheless may occasionally make an interesting or perceptive contribution to class discussion. Information can be gained both from the child and from others in the class. In fact, children are often the most aware of what each one of them is good at. Information can be sought through general discussion in class, one-to-one informal talks and interviews, evidence from Records of Achievement and through 'thinking' or 'learning' logs in which children reflect on their own learning (O'Brien 1998a).

The impact of learning difficulties

Some highly able and talented children may not be able to demonstrate their potential because of impediments to their learning. They may have a specific difficulty in relation to literacy (dyslexia) that interferes with their ability to read easily or to write and spell correctly. They may have a physical or sensory impairment that limits their movement or their ability to take in information or to demonstrate their understanding as readily as those without such difficulties. They may have difficulty in expressing themselves because of a lack of control over the physical mechanics of speech or they may lack the muscle control necessary for recording their ideas and or for the practical work that would demonstrate their understanding and creativity. Some may suffer from particular language and communication disorders which affect a wide area of language development and social interaction. Children with learning difficulties in a particular aspect of their performance may still have advanced skills in other areas. In such situations it becomes especially important to be flexible and sensitive in the way the children's efforts are assessed, and there is an increased need to look for many sources of information that might provide further insight into the children's potential capabilities.

CHAPTER 9

Provision within the school: policy and organisation

Terminology

The government's Excellence in Cities initiative uses the term 'Gifted and Talented' to describe the group of pupils for whom schools are expected to make additional provision. Procedures are set out for identifying the pupils who should qualify for inclusion in the Gifted and Talented programme. All the related documents, as well as DfES and Ofsted documentation, now use Gifted and Talented as the standard terminology.

But the G & T pupils, as they are now being called, are neither a discrete nor a homogeneous group. There are no cut-off points on the scale of human intelligence and performance, no legitimate levels at which we can say that one person can be categorised and given a special label. In schools making special provision for 'Gifted and Talented' children there will be a number of pupils who have not been identified and included within the G & T group but who are equally able. Inclusion within the group may depend on fairly arbitrary decisions based on given percentages or availability of resources. We also know that there are many very able and talented pupils in our schools who are not being stretched and who are capable of achieving far more. Among these there are also pupils whose abilities are, or potentially could be, exceptional.

Language has an enormous influence on how we perceive the world and what meaning we construe on experiences. In Part 1 of this book we focused on children whose development is unusually precocious or where their abilities and talents mark them out as being 'exceptional'. The term exceptional was used in order to avoid the unhelpful connotations that can arise with the term gifted. Part 2 is concerned with 'provision' and teaching is inevitably at the centre of any educational provision. As we are dealing in the following chapters with teaching and learning issues, it is important to be able to encompass all children who may be working, or able to work, at a high level. Such children may or may not be exceptional in relation to their peers, but they may be experiencing frustration through a lack of appropriate learning opportunities. Their talents may not be being fully realised. In Part 2 the terminology to describe these pupils will therefore be changed to 'more able' and this will be taken to include both intellectual ability and all other talents.

Establishing a whole-school policy

Local Education Authorities are required to publish a statement of policy regarding the education of more able pupils. However, there is not the same obligation on schools. There is, in fact, no statutory requirement for schools to have a specific and separate written policy on their provision for more able pupils. The legislation for pupils with special educational needs and the SEN Code of Practice do not encompass the needs of more able pupils. However, in 1999 the Select Committee recommended that 'schools should have an explicit whole-school policy which sets out the principles and aims which underpin the provision and gives details of the arrangements made to meet the needs of pupils' (House of Commons Select Committee report 1999). Good practice would indicate that this is a sensible thing to do.

The education of children is a whole-school responsibility. Teachers need to be clear about the aims and policies of the school and to be able to work within an agreed framework. Evidence suggests that where there is a clear written policy, supported by governors, parents and teachers, the importance of attending to the individual needs of pupils permeates every aspect of school life. No longer does the education and support of a child with particular needs remain the responsibility of individual teachers. The very process of consultation and discussion that leads to the drawing up of the policy itself can help staff clarify their own understandings and increase their commitment to the school's arrangements. A policy statement can also provide the framework for future developments of provision and for monitoring and evaluating the school's arrangements.

Some schools decide to use their special needs policy or their equal opportunities policy as a vehicle for their policy statements for more able pupils. There is some attraction to this approach as it places the needs of more able children firmly within the context of making provision for *all* children, taking account of individual circumstances. However, if everyone is to be clear about what is being provided, there will need to be specific reference to what arrangements are being made for more able children in the school as a whole and in each curriculum area. It will also be important to clarify specific responsibilities for auditing, coordinating and evaluating the provision, and for monitoring the progress of the children.

There are now many excellent examples of school policies available. Some are included in the many publications on the education of able children cited in the Reference sections (Eyre, 1997; Teare, 1997; Wallace, 2000). Others are included in manuals of guidance provided by LEAs, for instance by Bromley, Cheshire, Nottinghamshire and Hampshire, to name but a few. Some have been produced by individual schools. The National Association for Able Children in Education (NACE) also has a range of useful booklets on drawing up policies for very able children.

Pupil grouping

The evidence presented to the House of Commons Select Committee suggested that different patterns of organisation and ways of grouping pupils for teaching purposes could all be effective, if well managed. The Committee therefore concluded that 'There is no single best way to meet all these children's needs' (House of Commons Select Committee report 1999). Each type of arrangement has particular advantages as well as disadvantages for all children, including the more able.

Mixed-ability grouping

Mixed-ability grouping avoids the problem of selection and can, where it is well handled, provide a learning context in which children can develop at their own pace. Expectations of pupils' performance can be more open and the children are also less likely to suffer from being labelled. For more able children, learning in a mixed-ability context can ensure that they listen to a wide range of views and appreciate the different contributions that others can make to a task. It also diminishes the possibility that they will think of themselves as different from the rest. It can encourage them to recognise that learning is a shared activity and that they can benefit from and contribute to other people's ideas. However, where a teacher is not skilled in managing learning in a mixed-ability context, there is a risk that more able children may be required to repeat work with which they are already familiar or practise the same skill over and over again. As a result they can easily become bored and frustrated, or learn to suppress their opinions and knowledge if they receive adverse comments from their peers. They may be required to work alone for much of the time, lose their motivation to work hard or become accustomed to taking a dominant position in the group.

Setting or target grouping

Setting or target grouping has long been used in secondary schools as an approach to meeting the needs of pupils with different levels of ability. In recent years it has been increasingly used in primary schools, particularly for English and mathematics. It offers a more flexible approach than grouping whole classes by ability, as children can be moved between and across groups

Figure 9.1 'I don't care about your advanced computer course, Richard, we've still got a test on the three-times table this morning!'

for different subjects as their needs require. Setting has the advantage of making it easier for the teacher to match the work to the children's abilities. For more able children it provides the opportunity to work with others at a similar level and to meet the challenge of ideas as advanced as their own. However, even in setted arrangements the needs of more able children are likely to be different and some will be capable of working at a much higher level than the rest of the group. Teachers will still need to take account of the varying levels of ability. As far as the children are concerned, if all their learning takes place in setted groups then the quality and range of their learning will be more restricted. They will miss out on some important aspects of their overall development. Setting arrangements need to be balanced by other opportunities to work in contexts where ability is not the determining factor.

Streaming

Streaming involves selecting pupils for their all-round ability and teaching them as a whole group, or stream. It may provide children with opportunities to learn alongside others who are capable of working at a similar pace and level. However, the system has major drawbacks. Many more able pupils do not have all-round ability. And selection for a particular stream can, at best, be fairly arbitrary. The arrangements tend to be inflexible and create difficulties in accommodating children's differing rates of development. Streaming arrangements can also act as a discouragement to children, as those destined to lower streams can easily learn to think of themselves as non-achievers, second-class citizens in the school, unlikely to make good progress.

Working with an older age group

Children with exceptional ability in an area of learning, or where their needs can only be met through an individualised programme, can sometimes benefit from working with an older age group for some subjects. It is unlikely that such arrangements would be considered sensible for the majority of more able pupils, whose needs should be able to be met within the existing class arrangements. It is, however, more common in primary schools where there may be no other children of a similar age with whom the exceptional child can work at their own level and is therefore spending too much time working alone. In such circumstances, the chance to work with an older age group can provide a child with the opportunity to learn alongside others at an appropriate level, to move ahead at a faster pace and avoid the frustration or boredom of doing work that is too undemanding. The arrangements, however, can present problems for the school and the child, not the least of which is the question of timetabling. The child also risks being marked out and can become a target for unkind behaviour and comment from peers. Only in very exceptional circumstances is such a practice used in secondary schools. Setting or streaming is much more common.

CHAPTER 10

Provision within the school: teaching and learning

The National Curriculum

The National Curriculum has established an overall framework for children's learning. By setting out the levels of knowledge, skills and understanding for children in all subjects in the curriculum at each stage of their education, the National Curriculum provides a 'map' which schools and teachers can use when planning for pupils in different age ranges or at different stages in their learning. This makes it easier for teachers to plan for children with precocious levels of attainment, since the higher levels of working have been set out in some detail, providing teachers with a clear indication of the goals children can work towards. The 1999 revision to the National Curriculum Orders allows teachers to respond with more flexibility to the needs of pupils with different levels of ability. It increases the scope for teachers to provide children with appropriately challenging content and materials that can, if necessary, be selected from earlier or later Key Stages. Adaptations to the programmes of study can ensure that more able children can progress at their own pace and do not have to be held back by limitations within the curriculum.

However, just moving children ever onwards and upwards through the identified levels of learning is insufficient as the sole means of providing learning experiences. This is also a fairly crude approach to planning and managing the curriculum, creating major organisational difficulties as a child progresses through the educational system. It can also result in a child failing to establish an appropriate grounding of knowledge and understanding in a subject. *Teaching Scientifically Able Pupils in Primary Schools* and *Teaching Scientifically Able Pupils in Secondary Schools*, two very useful NACE publications, show, for example, how the National Curriculum topics in science can be mapped across the Key Stages and extended to cater for even the brightest pupils (O'Brien 1998a, 1998b). Effective teaching also needs to provide opportunities that cater for the full range of 'intelligences' described by Gardner (1983), not solely the linguistic and mathematical/logical intelligences that are so highly valued in western society. There have to be ways in which not only different levels of ability but also different learning styles can be accommodated within the curriculum.

Common approaches to differentiation

Planning to meet the needs of more able children within the context of mixed-ability classrooms, or even in classes which have been set by ability, is not easy, especially if there is one child whose understanding and skills far surpass those of the rest of the class. Teachers have to ensure that the tasks they present to children do in fact challenge their thinking, and encourage them to produce work that *extends* their existing knowledge and skills. If work is set at the same level for the whole class, some children may struggle and lose confidence, while others may become bored and frustrated or learn to reduce their effort and output.

Teaching is a highly skilled and demanding activity, and in recent years teachers have been hard-pressed by the many changes and developments they have been required to introduce to their classrooms. Nevertheless, with care and imagination, appropriate and relevant learning opportunities can be planned for the great majority of able children, including those with exceptional abilities, within the context of their regular classrooms. Some of the more common approaches to differentiation include modifying the work through differences in:

- **Task:** Children can be given different tasks based on what they already know and can do. Tasks can be differentiated in terms of difficulty or degree of challenge
- **Outcome:** Children work on the same task but the teacher has different *expectations* for what they will achieve
- **Pace**: Children are given a common task but are given different lengths of *time* to complete it
- **Resources**: Children are set a common task but work with a range of different resources, some of which require a greater level of reading or research skills
- **Input**: Children are given the same task but some will have more detailed instructions, whereas others may have only minimal guidance
- **Information**: Children are set a common task but the kind of information they work with and the texts they use may be different, with some children being expected to handle more complex information and concepts
- **Choice**: Children are given choice in what tasks they undertake or how they handle the content of the learning task
- **Open-ended tasks**: Children work on a task for which there is no particular right answer or outcome and each is then free to explore different approaches
- **Alternative ways of recording:** Children are encouraged to record their work in a variety of ways, some of which may require a higher level of imagination, performance or skill
- **Role**: Children work on the same task but each is given a particular role, some of which are more demanding than others, including the task of teaching a skill or process to others
- **Grouping**: Children have a common task but are grouped according to ability and expected to perform at a level appropriate to their ability
- **Homework:** Children are set different kinds or amounts of homework according to their abilities and interests.

(adapted from suggestions in Eyre 1997)

Structuring the learning

There are now a number of textbooks and handbooks that provide practical advice for planning for more able pupils in ways that are manageable within the classroom. It is not within the scope of this book to provide extensive detail on classroom provision and teaching strategies which have been so comprehensively described elsewhere (see Reference sections). However, it is worth highlighting two approaches that have been found to be particularly effective by teachers when planning for a range of levels of challenge in any classroom activity.

The first is Bloom's Taxonomy. Bloom identified characteristics of different levels of thinking which he placed in a hierarchical order from the simplest to the most complex and demanding (Bloom 1956). The six levels are:

- **Knowledge** (the ability to recall information and facts)
- **Comprehension** (the ability to make sense of information, to understand)
- **Application** (the ability to demonstrate understanding, to use knowledge and apply it in different contexts)
- **Analysis** (the ability to see patterns, identify components and recognise meanings)
- **Synthesis** (the ability to generalise from given facts, relating knowledge from several areas, and predicting and drawing conclusions)
- **Evaluation** (the ability to compare, discriminate, assess and reach reasoned judgements).

Table 10.1 Bloom's Taxonomy

SKILLS	BEHAVIOUR
KNOWLEDGE:	Demonstrating knowledge of facts, figures, information, Observation, Recall,...
COMPREHENSION:	Understanding, Explaining, Comparing, Contrasting, Interpreting, Ordering,...
APPLICATION:	Using knowledge, methods, concepts, Solving problems,...
ANALYSIS:	Recognising patterns, components, hidden meanings, Identifying themes, key issues, connections,...
SYNTHESIS:	Relating, Generalising, Bringing information together from different sources, Combining, Predicting, Concluding,...
EVALUATION:	Comparing, Discriminating, Prioritising, Verifying, Assessing, Finding alternatives, Suggesting improvements,...

Bloom suggested that the first three, Knowledge, Comprehension and Application are what he called 'Lower-order' thinking skills. Analysis, Synthesis and Evaluation, on the other hand, are higher-order skills and are more intellectually demanding.

Bloom's ideas have been successfully adapted for use in classrooms and for planning different levels of intellectual challenge within individual activities. Using the structure teachers can plan for:

- different levels of challenge *within* each category (requiring from some children more generalised knowledge, more specialised knowledge, deeper understanding, more examples, further ways of applying the knowledge, new patterns, more detailed analysis, more varied or more complex ways of relating ideas, broader or more interesting ways of comparing, assessing, evaluating)
- giving different *emphasis* or weight to particular categories according to different needs and abilities (requiring some pupils to spend more time on analysis, synthesis or evaluation of the core task, on the assumption that mastery of knowledge and comprehension will have been more easily acquired)
- allocating aspects of tasks that require different levels of challenge to particular pupils (when pupils are engaged in a group activity that involves a variety of tasks, some may undertake those aspects that require higher-order thinking skills, such as researching, assessing or prioritising information, while others may contribute through more practical ways).

Table 10.2 Using Bloom's Taxonomy to plan a learning task

Planning for a topic on plants	
Knowledge:	Name the plant
Comprehension:	What is the function of each part of the plant?
Application:	Compare the shape, size, colour of plants
Analysis:	Why are seeds of flowers that shape? (dispersal, pollination)
Synthesis:	Design a plant for different locations/purposes
Evaluation:	Which plant will grow best in particular conditions or locations?

The second approach is based on a model for planning for different needs within the classroom proposed by Brahm Norwich (1996). Norwich suggests teachers consider the learning needs of children in terms of three categories: *common* needs (those that affect all the pupils), *exceptional* needs (those that affect particular groups of pupils, such as those with literacy difficulties, hearing impairment and so on) and *individual* needs (those that are special to a particular pupil, such as a child who is traumatised by a home circumstance, or a child who requires a special piece of equipment).

Using this approach, teachers can plan tasks for groups of children and for individuals using a structure of: MUST, SHOULD, COULD. If, to avoid confusion, the term 'exceptional' is replaced by the term 'additional', more able children might be grouped within the categories of *common* needs and *additional* needs, whereas a child with exceptional ability might be considered to have *common* needs and *individual* needs. So, in deciding what activities the class would carry out during the study of a particular topic the teacher might expect that *all* the class 'Must'... (learn the names, study, record, list, write...), *some* children 'Should'... (practise, work on more examples, write a more extensive account...); and *certain* children 'Could'... (research, seek alternatives, review...). A model such as this allows for flexibility to be readily incorporated into all planning, and enables interesting and challenging activities to be offered to children with a very wide range of abilities.

Table 10.3 Planning for differentiated activities for a topic on homes (Gwen Goodhew)

MUST	SHOULD	COULD
Look at local homes	Find local examples of different house types,...	Compare local houses, analyse features, compare costs, evaluate market values in different localities
Talk about differences	Use technical terms: high-rise, tenement, detached, semi-detached, Housing Association,...	Find homes suitable for different needs: the elderly, single people, families. Explain why, identify availability, shortages,...
Collect, illustrate,...	Observe different styles, features and materials used in a range of local houses	Explore, research architectural styles and features at different periods in history

Developing children's thinking

While the National Curriculum may provide a useful framework for planning the curriculum, it is the way that teachers work with their pupils that determines how children progress and how effective they become as learners.

Much teaching is didactic in nature. With a heavy programme of work to cover, and so much emphasis given to knowledge and content in the curriculum, there is a very real risk that children's natural curiosity will be stifled early in their school career, and that they will become accustomed to being 'receivers' rather than 'active participants'. If we want children to develop lively enquiring minds, to question, reflect, discriminate, judge and make well-informed decisions, we need to help them develop the necessary 'tools'. We need to provide them with the skills for thinking, researching and solving problems.

For children with exceptional abilities a skills-based approach to learning is of special value, since they often acquire knowledge at a rapid rate. Activities can be structured to call upon higher-order skills, as was illustrated through the use of Bloom's Taxonomy. Teaching can also be planned to ensure that children are able to use the full range of Gardner's multiple intelligences rather than being asked to rely too heavily on linguistic, mathematical and logical reasoning skills.

Furthermore, a research study into children's learning found that in very able pupils, existing knowledge is highly interconnected and new knowledge is immediately linked to prior knowledge and experience. However, it also appeared that far too few opportunities were given to students to capitalise on these skills (Resnick 1989). Other studies into effective learning highlight the importance of students being given opportunities to reflect on their own learning (Kolb and Fry 1975). According to Kolb and Fry, learning is conceived as a four-staged cycle. Immediate concrete experience is the basis for observation and reflection, which are then assimilated into a theory from which new implications for action can be drawn. These implications, or hypotheses, lead to decisions about what new experiences are needed.

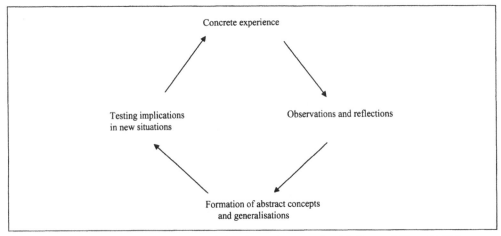

Figure 10.1 Kolb's description of the learning cycle (Kolb and Fry 1975)

However, some more able children may not be able to organise and apply their learning in an orderly or efficient way. All students can be helped to become more effective in their learning by being encouraged to reflect on the strategies they use and analysing the degree to which different approaches or actions helped or hindered them to achieve their goals (Thomas and Harri-Augstein 1985). An approach to helping students acquire this 'self-reflection' skill is outlined in Chapter 11. Specific teaching of research skills and approaches to problem-solving can also provide the structures through which children develop greater independence and autonomy. This frees them to work at a pace and at a level that best suit their abilities.

Teaching thinking

'Thinking is a skill and, like a skill, it can be developed and improved if one knows how' (De Bono 1970). De Bono claimed that lateral thinking is closely related to insight, creativity and humour but, unlike these three, it is a skill that can be taught.

We have already discussed how children's thinking skills can be specifically encouraged through planning tasks and activities that extend the demand of the lower-order thinking skills as well as calling for the use of the higher-order skills of analysis, synthesis and evaluation. Other approaches can also train children to extend and stretch their thinking muscles and broaden the base of their existing experience. Instrumental Enrichment, a scheme devised by the Israeli psychologist Reuven Feuerstein to teach thinking skills, is still used in some schools today (Feuerstein 1980). Structured approaches more commonly used include De Bono's CoRT Thinking programme, Blagg et al.'s Somerset Thinking Skills Project and Lake's Primary Thinking Skills Project (De Bono 1970; Ballinger et al. 1988; Lake 1990). All three provide thinking and discussion exercises that encourage pupils to think more creatively, imaginatively and logically. De Bono's CoRT Thinking programme, using a snappy set of acronyms (CAF: Consider All Factors; PMI: Plus, Minus, Interesting; C&S: Consequences and Sequels, etc.), presents children with topics for discussion that force them to look beyond the first response and encourage them to avoid being trapped in narrow ways of viewing events (De Bono 1970). The exercises have mainly been used with older pupils in secondary schools, but can just as effectively be introduced to younger children. They are fun to practise, and once children become familiar with the strategies they can readily and rapidly apply them at relevant moments in a discussion or in planning and reviewing work. The Somerset Thinking Skills programme has been equally successful in primary schools (Ballinger et al. 1998).

Teaching subject-specific thinking skills has also been found to be an effective way of raising achievement not only in the subject itself but also in improving performance across the curriculum. Many secondary schools have introduced the 'Cognitive Acceleration through Science Education' course (CASE) with excellent results. A programme for primary-aged pupils has now been developed. A similar course for secondary mathematics is also available: 'Cognitive Acceleration through Mathematics' (CAME).

A quite different approach is taken in such developments as the adaptation of the American-based programme Philosophy for Children, introduced into this country by Karen Murris, and by Robert Fisher, at Brunel University. This has resulted in some highly promising work in a number of schools. The approach was developed by Maurice Lipman, an American philosopher who uses philosophy to create a 'Community of Enquiry', in which 'socratic' discussion forms the basis for developing children's thinking and reasoning skills. Children develop their understanding and learn to attribute 'meaning' through thinking and testing their ideas against others (Lipman 1991). The Thinking Skills materials and the philosophy and practice that underpin the Community of Enquiry approach to learning, described by Murris and Fisher, have particular potential for children who want to explore at a high level but who need to learn to appreciate the thinking, contribution and aspirations of others (Murris 1992; Fisher 1995).

A comprehensive approach to teaching thinking would include a mixture of structured, creative, problem-solving and critical thinking. To achieve this a school would need to offer structured programmes taught as additional to the normal curriculum, subject-specific thinking skills programmes, and to develop thinking skills across the curriculum.

Enrichment

'By using a variety of methods, both within the school and outside, effective provision for able and talented children can be greatly enhanced' (Teare 1997).

Enrichment activities are those that widen the experience of children and thereby enhance their overall learning. Enrichment activities 'go beyond the regular curriculum'. They may have no direct link to the main programmes of study but may aim to provide opportunities for children to think more broadly and widen their horizons. In his book *Effective Provision for Able and Talented Children*, Teare suggests that enrichment activities can be offered at different levels and in a variety of ways. Enrichment activities can be:

- open to all children, but not necessarily be designed to challenge the most able
- broadening experiences for a wide range of children but which also offer opportunities for the most able to perform at the highest level (music, theatre, art)
- specifically directed to more able children (seminars, projects).

(Teare 1997)

Many enrichment activities can take place within the normal curriculum in school, through adapting the tasks or the working arrangements for groups of children and individuals. Both Deborah Eyre in her book *Able Children in Ordinary Schools* as well as Teare suggest a number of ways as to how this can take place (Eyre 1997; Teare 1997). They suggest that additional opportunities for enrichment can be provided by such activities as: teaching an additional subject or course, special events where the normal timetable is suspended, competitions, seminars, specialist workshops, interest clubs, residencies with guest performers, after-school and weekend events, and summer schools.

Summer schools, where nominated groups of pupils are given opportunities to take part in specially designed events during the summer holidays, are now part of a nationwide development, funded by the government, to broaden the range of specialist experiences for pupils deemed 'Gifted and Talented'. Other activities may take place out of school and in conjunction with other schools or members of the community. The Excellence in Cities initiative includes arrangements for such collaborative events designed for the most able pupils in the area.

Individual Education Plans

Individual Education Plans, introduced by the *Code of Practice* 1994 for pupils with special educational needs, have raised awareness about the importance of paying additional attention to the needs and progress of pupils who have difficulties with their learning. They have acted as the catalyst for planning and reviewing the school's arrangements, and for ensuring that there is a coherent approach to any special or additional provision. The structures and procedures provide a suitable way of planning for any pupil for whom flexible arrangements are needed, including pupils who are exceptionally able and talented. The great majority of more able pupils do not have 'difficulties' with their learning and behaviour. However, some do, especially if they have difficulties related to literacy skills, or physical or sensory impairments. When this is the case an Individual Education Plan can be useful in clearly identifying and recording their needs and specifying how the school will help them overcome their difficulty and make progress.

A few children's development may be so unusual as to warrant special arrangements. In such cases, an Individual Education Plan can legitimise alternative activities or the involvement of people from outside the school. For instance, arrangements can be set out in the pupil's plan for a child or young person to follow a course of study other than that of their peer group, such as may happen where a secondary-aged pupil is entered early for external examinations or follows an Open University course. Where additional opportunities are made available through the school's extra-curricular programme, these too can be included as part of the overall provision that will meet an individual pupil's needs. Individual Education Plans can identify the resources and sources of support that can be made available where people are prepared to be flexible and creative, and are willing to work together. The central tenet in drawing up an individual plan is the involvement of the pupil and the parents in helping identify the child's needs and in agreeing on ways of meeting them. This requires pupils, teachers and parents to set targets and to meet regularly to review progress. Such processes have great potential for raising pupil motivation and encouraging responsibility for their own learning.

Avoiding the 'lone-ranger' syndrome in the primary school

Ensuring that all children in the class are meaningfully occupied throughout the period of time that has been planned for an activity requires careful planning and skilful organisation. A teacher who is unprepared for a child who works much faster than others and who needs very little help with the tasks may resort to giving the child time-filler activities: another book to read, another exercise, more of the same. This can quickly sap the child's enthusiasm and does little to encourage them to work as hard next time. Alternatively, the busy teacher may be only too thankful to be able to send a capable child to work on their own. If the teacher is not careful such children may find themselves working far too often and for far too long in isolation, and developing a 'lone-ranger on the desert of life' syndrome.

Modern technology, if it is not sensitively managed, can sometimes exacerbate the isolation. A very bright child may become a very lonely child. Ironically, despite the fact that exceptional children may need as much opportunity for personal contact as any other child, if not more, in order to maintain their interest and excitement in learning, they may not be given as much attention. Two rather serious consequences may follow. By spending so much time working on their own such children may come to regard all learning as a solitary pursuit, instead of what it should be: a shared activity, an exciting process based on communication. The children may become increasingly unable to work, or play, with others. The more 'knowledge' they acquire the greater the distance between themselves and their companions, and the greater the difficulty in believing that other children can be sources of interest and pleasure. In fact, when interviewed as young adults, some very able students described the problems they now experience as a result of never having learned to chat or engage in small talk, and never having developed friendships and easy working relationships with children of the same age.

Teachers need to be aware of these risks and to monitor carefully the amount of time children spend on independent learning. 'Children need to learn how to collaborate in order to collaborate to learn,' says Professor Wood (1999). Teachers should therefore create opportunities for paired and group tasks in which different levels of competence can be of value rather than a problem. Pupils can be paired for research work, and for work on computer programs. Thematic project work can provide a flexible base for such cooperation between children. Stories need not only be produced by individuals, but can also be developed in groups. Activities can be devised which call upon all class members to contribute, that are based on interests rather than dependent on skills and which highlight the sharing of experiences and the mutuality of feelings. Other arrangements might include:

- 'Jigsaw' groups: Each member is given a particular aspect of a task to carry out or research and they come together after an agreed time to produce their group product or findings
- 'Rainbow' groups: Each group is given a different aspect of a task to work on together. New groups are then formed, composed of one child from each original group, and the findings are pooled
- Shared characteristic groups: Groups are formed on the basis of some shared characteristic (same sex, birth position, cultural experiences) to discuss topics from a particular perspective before coming together as a class to identify similarities and differences.

In a context where the contribution of each child is important to the group's outcome, the special abilities of very bright children can be welcomed by their peers, rather than resulting in a negative response.

While time must be found for all children to have individual contact with an adult this does not always have to be with the teacher. A wealth of talent and enthusiasm exists among parents and within the community at large. Many people welcome the opportunity to give time to meeting with individuals or small groups of children. Nowadays most schools embrace the help available from parents, from community volunteers and from older pupils taking part in work experience, or where this forms part of their course work for GCSE, GNVQ or General Studies. Sixth-form students can befriend younger pupils, and act as mentors in specialist subjects. Contacts can be arranged with local colleges and universities where students may also be interested in supporting pupils with particular interests. Many a child's continued enthusiasm for learning has been founded on the early provision of such mentors and friends. These possibilities will be discussed at greater length in Chapters 11 and 12. A school that welcomes the contributions that a whole community can make towards the education and development of its children is in a good position for being able to meet the needs of even the most exceptional children.

Additional opportunities in the school

The formal curriculum provides the platform for teacher planning and pupil learning in the classroom. But the whole-school experience provides many other opportunities for building on, extending and enriching the quality of children's learning. Schools that aim to provide for the diverse range of needs and interests of *all* their pupils try to ensure a degree of choice and flexibility which supplements the core educational provision. Traditionally, this has been accepted practice for children with special needs or learning difficulties where special programmes are organised to help pupils develop their social skills, or where additional experiences may be provided to encourage their independence. Additional or alternative teaching arrangements may be made and, in Key Stage 4, courses leading to sources of accreditation other than GCSE are often included in the school's overall curriculum provision. Such flexibility is equally appropriate for more able children or, more usually, for those with exceptional ability. In addition to the normal practice of modifying classroom work, some schools organise tutorial groups, drawing together pupils with similar interests or levels of learning for extension work in particular subjects. Others set up lunch-time and after-school clubs or arrange 'seminar groups' for pupils interested in discussing challenging issues. Other special arrangements include annual competitions for science or technology projects, special 'enrichment' days or residential courses for advanced specialist work in different subjects. The ethos and the quality of a school is often defined by these 'additional' opportunities which demonstrate a whole community commitment to the development of pupils as individuals as well as promoting their shared needs and interests.

CHAPTER 11

Pastoral care and support

Understanding the issues

Part 1 explored in some detail the issues that may arise when children's development is precocious or where their level of understanding and skill is far in advance of that of their peers. The evidence shows how difficult it can be for these children to form friendships with children of their own age and how vulnerable they can become to being rejected by their peer group. It is understandable how they can easily become bored and frustrated in class and this in turn poses a danger for the development of poor attitudes to learning and an inappropriate self-concept. It can be seen that some children develop a punishing self-image where success in their work becomes inextricably embedded in their feeling of self-worth, producing a fear of failure that may result in the need to strive continually to be a top performer at all times. Children who are prevented from demonstrating or using their abilities because of the limiting effect of a disability or through some other personal circumstances are especially at risk.

The great majority of more able children, including those with exceptional ability, progress well in school and do not suffer any particular difficulties in their social relationships. The stresses and strains they experience are part and parcel of the normal processes of growing up. Freeman (2001) confirmed this in her research study which tracked 210 children, from primary age into adulthood. Of these children, 82 had IQs that placed them in the 'gifted' range. When compared with the young people in the sample group whose IQ placed them in the 'above average' or the 'about average' range, the group with the highest IQs did not, as a whole, demonstrate any marked differences in their general welfare or development, or in their social relationships. However, in all three groups, there were individuals who had not prospered. Some had opted out of academic work and not continued their studies into further or higher education, or had not achieved success in other areas of their lives. Others had become lonely and isolated individuals. Of itself, therefore, high intelligence as measured by the IQ cannot be said to bring about emotional problems. The results of Freeman's study suggest that it is other factors in life that determine how well a person develops. In the case of the young people in the study, much had depended on the sensitivity of the teachers and the support they had received as pupils in school. Even more important had been the nature and quality of the support from home. Where parents had been able to keep a sense of perspective about their child's abilities and talents, had been able to provide them with adequate space and resources, and where they had been actively 'involved' through encouragement without undue pressure, the young people had, on the whole, done well (Freeman 2001).

Where children and young people are clearly having difficulties with their work and relationships, it is important to try to understand what lies behind their problems and work with them to find acceptable solutions.

Underachievement

To a certain extent everyone underachieves. We could no doubt all do a great deal better given different circumstances, more help, less hassle and more favourable conditions. Underachievement is a strange concept since it assumes that someone else knows better than you what you could or should be doing or able to do.

However, teachers and parents are understandably concerned where children appear not to be fully engaged with their learning or are not making the progress that might be expected. Schools are increasingly directing their efforts to ensure that all pupils are achieving as well as they could and looking for ways in which help can be given to those who, for whatever reason, seem to have lost interest or motivation to do well.

The reasons for underachievement are many and sometimes very complex. They may be to do with family circumstances, emotional problems or partly to do with the child's personality. The child may not enjoy hard work and may prefer to take a low-key approach to life. In a study on underachievement, linked factors included poor motor control affecting the child's performance, lack of parental interest in the child's education, family breakdown and low expectations from parents and teachers (Gottfried *et al.* 1994). Other factors known to affect achievement include: poverty, frequent changes of schools attended, the appropriateness of work, undetected specific learning difficulties, lack of cooperation between home and school, and gender issues (Lee-Corbin and Denicolo 1998; Freeman 2001). More able children and those with exceptional abilities and talents may have learned to switch off as a result of boredom and frustration early in their school lives. Or they may have chosen to disguise their abilities in an effort to be acceptable among their peer group.

Underachievement is very hard to tackle. It is especially difficult where such a culture has developed in the school or among the peer group, and where to work hard is seen as not 'cool'. Many schools are faced with a very real challenge in encouraging pupils to recognise the value in achieving at the highest level. In such circumstances more able children struggle to survive. However, where teachers and parents are prepared to work with the children and their peers to find a solution, there is evidence that the problems can be overcome. In her first follow-up study of gifted children at the age of 18, Freeman found that some of the factors that had contributed to the progress of 'successful' able children were: parental pressure that did not put too much pressure on the child, freedom from domestic stress, appropriate encouragement and teaching at school, no obligation to conform to the average but freedom to develop in their own way, encouragement to make their own decisions, and respect for their abilities (Freeman 1991b). While the domestic stress may not be easily resolved, it should be possible to work on the other 'supporting' factors. Whitmore, in a research study, found that underachievement could be successfully tackled by providing a more stimulating curriculum with an emphasis on genuine success, together with direct work with children on enhancing their self-concept (Whitmore 1980, in Gottfried *et al.* 1994).

Strategies for supporting primary-aged children

In Chapter 5, when discussing children's needs, we saw how children learn best when they feel safe and secure in their classrooms and valued by their friends and their teachers. Teachers, therefore, need to ensure that in their classrooms, all children are made to feel welcome and become confident in themselves as successful learners. They can only do this if they create a 'climate', or an 'ethos', in which the contributions of everyone in the class are seen to be important. Teachers can help children feel valued through:

- looking for ways in which each child can contribute to the work of the class as a whole
- providing challenging and interesting work that children can undertake with others of similar ability
- encouraging children to set their own goals and to share in the critical evaluation of their own work as well as that of others
- showing interest and respect for the children's ideas
- actively seeking to resolve any difficulties that may have arisen in the children's social relationships or in the way they are responding to their work.

Strategies for supporting adolescents

Young people need support from adults to help them find a way through some of the challenges they meet in adolescence. But it must be support that recognises their growing maturity and respects their need to find personal solutions to problems. This is not always easy for either parents or teachers, as we are so used to directing and controlling, and to leading children along ways that we believe to be most suitable. Shifting the balance in our relationships so that young people take ownership of their lives and learning during adolescence, allowing them the freedom to risk making mistakes in the search for solutions, are some of the major challenges for parents and teachers. We have to guide without imposing, support without taking away the challenge. But additional support may be necessary for some individuals. This can often be done most effectively through tutoring and the use of mentors.

Tutoring

Staff in schools encourage pupils to take responsibility for their work in many different ways. 'Records of Achievement', with their emphasis on personal target-setting and review, play an important role in this. However, when used routinely, the process of setting objectives can become ineffective for the adults and meaningless for the pupils.

Many young people respond well to a 'self-organised' approach based on the work of Laurie Thomas and Sheila Harri-Augstein, two psychologists at Brunel University. Their work is founded on the theory of Personal Constructs developed by George Kelly, and has proven successful in a wide variety of settings in which people learn to become more effective in how they learn and what they do. 'Self-Organised Learning' is an approach based on structured conversations between tutor and student, which are called 'learning conversations'. These conversations help students develop a language for talking about their own learning. As a result, they become better able to reflect on and analyse what they are thinking and doing, and so learn to evaluate the effectiveness of their personal strategies for resolving problems (Thomas and Harri-Augstein 1985).

The learning conversations follow a set pattern through which the tutor, or 'learning coach', and the student discuss what the latter needs or wants to achieve (the *Purpose*). They explore the various ways in which the student may set about the task (the *Strategies*). They then consider what the student expects as an outcome and the criteria that will be used to judge success (the *Outcome*). The final phase (the *Review*) takes place after the activity or piece of work has been completed. The learning coach and the student track back through each of the previous stages and decide how successful or otherwise the process had been.

The tutor's role is to help the students clarify and 'own' what it is they intend to do and then to choose the strategies *they* think will best achieve their objectives. Students are far more likely to commit themselves and put an effort into something they want to do. They are more likely to give up if they have not recognised for themselves the value of what they are trying to do, or they have been told to do something in a particular way. We learn most effectively when we have some choice over how we do things, but are also helped to explore the many possible alternative strategies that could be used. At a later date, when the tutor and student come together to review what has been achieved, the tutor helps the student identify the factors that have contributed to the success or failure of a particular course of action. Through exploring, planning and reviewing in a structured way, such learning conversations can alter from being something that takes place between a tutor and the student to a process that takes place within the student's own head.

The value of using such an approach with more able students and those with exceptional abilities lies in the independence that can be given to the students in making decisions about how, where and when they work. It offers the potential for developing a more flexible way of working, and for sustaining motivation. It also enables a wider group of people to support students in their learning as it is not necessary to have specialist subject knowledge to be an effective tutor.

Mentoring

Mentoring has become a regular feature in many secondary schools as a means of tackling underachievement. Increasingly, mentors are being used to support children in primary schools as well. However, the role of mentor is not universally understood and there are many variations in the way the term has been interpreted. It is not always clear whether mentors should take a 'teacher-like' role and instruct, persuade or lead the pupil towards improvements in their motivation or learning, or whether they are to act as 'tutor' in the Self-Organised Learning sense of the term, or just to be a role model and friend. Mentors can be drawn from the staff or older pupils in the school or, as members of the local community, be invited to contribute to the school's arrangements for pupil support. Mentors for more able or exceptional pupils might also include undergraduates or post-graduate students from local universities. This might be of particular benefit for pupils from families or communities where there is no tradition of higher education.

To be effective, mentors need to be clear about the purpose of their involvement with a particular pupil and, ideally, to have received some training for their role. There needs to be an explicit agreement about the nature, timing and duration of the contact. Where the mentor's role is focused on raising the level of the pupils' academic achievement or providing them with opportunities to develop their thinking at a higher level than is currently possible in the classroom, they can:

- help the pupil identify and work on areas of the curriculum in which improvement is needed
- provide individual support for advanced level work
- explore subject-specific topics which may or may not be part of the main scheme of work
- work on challenging research projects that broaden the range of the pupil's experience.

Mentors need to be able to use a range of skills in questioning, challenging and support and to be able to develop a good relationship with the pupil.

More able pupils and those with exceptional abilities often develop interests that are hard for others to appreciate or share. Their sense of isolation can be exacerbated by the lack of opportunity to discuss their experiences and hobbies. They may be unable to exercise their artistic or sporting talents fully within the provision of the school. Their understanding and skills in a given subject area may have outstripped the ability of their teachers to provide help. For many such children a mentor can provide a life-line. Out in the community there are people who would enjoy giving time to a young person, having an opportunity to share common interests or to allow the young person to join them in their work. Mentors may be able to play an important part in repairing bruised self-esteem, or in restoring a disillusioned pupil's motivation for study. They can provide young people with valuable role models, raise their personal expectations, broaden their horizons and introduce them to a wider circle of people with similar interests. Mentors can also provide that invaluable additional personal time which is so difficult for many schools to provide from within their own resources.

Involving the pupils

One of the best ways to find out how to improve the provision being made in schools is to ask the pupils. All too often this valuable source of information is overlooked. Teachers talk to one another, consult with people from outside the school, audit resources and analyse results. It is rare for the children to be asked how the school's provision and practice helps them. Pupils may be asked their opinion about practical things and about the extra-curricular activities they might like to have on offer, but if teachers want to know how to help young people learn more effectively, they have to be prepared to ask the children about the teaching itself and the quality of personal support. Given the opportunity, young people are usually very helpful and responsive. When staff in one school decided to interview sixth-form students about their past experience they found they had to revise a number of assumptions about the school's provision. They asked the students how they learned best, what prevented them from doing their best work, in what ways the school could help them achieve better, and what changes they would make to alter the situation for pupils who were disaffected. The students emphasised the importance of firm management, high expectations, clear targets, constructive and honest commentary, fair treatment and plenty of opportunities for active participation. They also highlighted their need to work together in groups as well as to be given work to do on their own. Importantly, they identified areas of the school where practice needed attention, and gave constructive suggestions on how to tackle the culture of underachievement among boys. As a result a number of changes were implemented including more opportunities for pupils to take responsibility for their work, homework and extension work clubs, and the identification of a member of staff to monitor the progress and provision for high achievers (Leyden 1995).

Involvement of students in this way has great potential for creating a learning environment that fosters achievement, in which everyone feels they have a part to play, and where differences are valued for their contribution to the rich diversity of the community.

CHAPTER 12

Partnership and collaboration

Partnership with parents

The vital role of parents

Partnership with parents is now a priority in schools. Parents are recognised as having a vital role to play in the education of their child and in supporting the work of the school. After all, for most pupils, parents are the one constant factor in their lives; teachers come and go, others contribute at different times along the way, but parents accompany their children throughout their journey through school. Parents have the kind of detailed knowledge about their children that can help teachers understand young people's particular needs, what they enjoy and do well, and what makes them anxious. In addition, parents in homes where English is a second language may be able to provide important information on talents and interests that pupils may not be able to demonstrate at school. Bringing up children and helping them develop their abilities and skills is a shared responsibility, where each person has their own role to play and contribution to make. This sharing of responsibility is especially important where children may have special or additional needs. In such cases, parents need to feel confident that their child's needs are recognised and understood, and will be taken into account when planning what needs to be done to support the child's progress.

All schools inform parents about their children's progress. Termly, twice yearly or annual reports provide parents with a general and a more detailed account of what the children have achieved during the year and indicate where improvements could be made. Parents meetings also provide a forum for reviewing children's progress and these can provide valuable opportunities for meeting teachers face to face to talk about the children's work. However, the setting and time limitations do not always create the best context for a proper sharing of information or for exploring any real concerns. In the·past, many such meetings were very much a 'one-way' affair, with the emphasis being more on information-giving than information-sharing. This can still be the case today.

Figure 12.1 A meaningful exchange of information and views

Schools are usually very willing to arrange for additional meetings to discuss any particular matters of concern. However, it is not yet universal practice for schools to have arrangements in place that ensure they are kept regularly informed by parents about their children's interests, their needs and any individual circumstances that may be affecting their progress. This is easier to arrange in primary schools where parents and teachers can meet on a regular, even daily, basis and exchange information. It is also easier for primary teachers to get to know the children more intimately and to be more aware of individual circumstances and needs. In secondary schools such meetings have to scheduled and are therefore bound to be somewhat less frequent and more formal. They are also more likely only to occur when a problem arises or when either the school or the parents have a concern they wish to discuss.

Even where no special problems have arisen, parents may want to be sure that the school is aware of their child's abilities and that these are being taken into account in teachers' planning and monitoring. The school needs also to be aware of some of the issues that face parents whose children's development is any way unusual and be ready to support them in any way they can. While it is generally recognised that home factors may impinge on children's behaviour and learning in school, teachers may not always be aware of the impact of the classroom and the playground on the children's well-being and behaviour at home.

Issues for parents

There are a number of ways in which being the parent of a child with precocious or unusual abilities and talents can affect the relationship between home and school. Parents may themselves find it difficult to cope at home with a child who is unusually active and demanding. They may be finding it hard to handle jealousies within the family and find they are giving too much attention to one or other of their children. They may be confused by the erratic or uneven nature of their child's development. They may worry that the child is not being offered a suitable programme of education in school and attribute this to difficulties in the home.

In the early years, if their child is very demanding and finding it hard to make friends, parents may fear that teachers and others will attribute this to poor parenting skills. If their child becomes bored with work in school and begins to lose interest, parents are bound to want to intervene. However, if parents raise this as a concern with teachers, they may also be anxious about being labelled as 'pushy' parents.

Sometimes the school's response to parental anxieties results in misunderstandings. Teachers who believe that parents doubt their ability to teach their child properly may feel threatened and take defensive positions. Conversely, parents can feel threatened if they feel teachers consider they have unrealistic expectations of their child. Mismatches can occur between the teacher's and the parents' perception of a child's needs. For instance, a mother may believe her son is bored and need more stimulating activities, whereas the teacher may be worried about the child's poor concentration. A father may fear his daughter's ability has not been recognised, whereas the teacher may consider the child is being put under too much pressure to achieve (Lee-Corbin and Denicolo 1998). In her seminal writings about relationships between home and school, Elsie Osborne talks about 'Circular Causality' (Osborne 1994). She shows, for example, how the perceptions of both parties can be true at the same time and impact on one another, creating a 'circular' sequence of events. In the example above, the boy may not be able to concentrate very long on any one activity, but placing too much emphasis on improving his concentration skills may result in the child becoming increasingly resistant and telling his parents he is bored. The mother, in turn, by demanding more stimulating activities, may reinforce the teacher's belief that the parents are not taking sufficient account of the need to develop the child's ability to concentrate. As each side presses their point, they can all overlook what might lie at the heart of the problem.

Living with an adolescent can challenge any parent. It can be especially stressful if the young person's development is in any way unusual. Very able young people may find this period in their home and social lives very difficult to manage. They can find themselves becoming increasingly isolated if the gap between their own interests and those of their peers widens. Parents may find it difficult to understand what is happening, unsure about the best way to help, and reluctant to raise this with the school, lest their child be singled out as 'trouble'.

Even parents of young people who are apparently doing well and who are not socially isolated may fear that expectations have been set too low and that their child will not achieve the success they should in particular examinations. They can also worry if their child is not keeping a healthy balance between achievement and relaxation, between the hours spent on study compared to leisure pursuits (Gomme 2000).

When parents have a concern about their child, or wish to discuss their child's progress, they should do what they can to ensure that any meeting with school staff starts on a constructive footing. NACE has produced a useful booklet to help parents prepare for and manage the discussion. In it they warn against taking premature action when a problem arises. Parents are advised to get the whole story and check this with others. Then they should spend some time clarifying and defining the problem for themselves and gathering further evidence: what is bothering them or the child, why, how it is affecting the child's behaviour, what evidence do they have and what have they so far done about it? At the meeting they should explain, if at all possible, that they are not complaining but wanting to work with the school to resolve a problem. They should then decide together what the issues are, put forward the evidence they have from home and school, listen to each other's perspective and try to agree on a shared response (NACE: Parent Leaflet No. 2).

Parents as a resource

Parents play the most important part in their child's development. Their influence at home can make all the difference to how well a child does in school. The example they set can help their children develop and sustain an interest in learning and a balanced perspective of their own capabilities. They can also help their children to develop a sound approach to studying.

Bloom found that parents of 'successful' students:

- ensured that homework was completed before play
- helped the children organise their time
- showed disapproval of time being wasted
- put an emphasis on self-discipline
- involved their children in a range of activities
- demonstrated their pride in their children's achievements.

(Bloom 1985)

Freeman found a similar pattern of parental involvement with the more successful students in her research. She found that children also did well where parents:

- encouraged a variety of interests
- showed sensitivity to their child's interests and talents without trying to mould them to their own design
- provided the necessary materials and tuition to enable the child to pursue talents to a high standard
- helped children to discover what fun learning can be
- were able to judge when to intervene, when to apply some pressure and when to stand back.

(Lee-Corbin and Denicolo 1998)

Parents can help schools make sure that children are being offered the education and the guidance they need. They can help the school identify and plan provision for any special or additional needs, support the school's work through activities they do at home, and seek out materials, resources and sources of information that the school might find helpful for any enrichment programme. If a child's needs are so exceptional as to call for an Individual Educational Plan, then any special arrangements can be specified and the parents' role can also be included. The parents can then be confident that they will be involved in a regular review of their child's progress.

Links with the wider community

The challenge of educating and supporting our most able and talented children is not the sole responsibility of teachers in the child's own school and the parents. Schools may well need to look beyond their own institution and call upon the support of others in the community. There is a wealth of resources in the community which can be utilised to extend and enrich the provision for all children, including the more able.

The Excellence in Cities initiative has made the use of community resources an integral part of its arrangements. Gifted and Talented Coordinators oversee the developments in a cluster of schools and have a role in developing and coordinating additional provision in the area. Opportunities are provided for teachers from different schools to come together to share practice and develop new materials and strategies. Opportunities are also provided for the most able pupils in the area to take part in special enrichment activities. This is an excellent development and one that will provide valuable examples of collaboration for others to consider. However, there are already numerous examples of good practice, where schools have widened the boundaries of their provision to include support from many other sources.

Links with schools in the same phase

More able children and those with exceptional abilities benefit from the opportunity to engage from time to time with children of similar ability in activities that challenge them to the limit of their capabilities. This can be difficult to arrange in some schools, particularly in primary or rural schools or where the school is very small. The teachers in any one school may not have the specific expertise to extend a child's thinking fully in a subject or a skill. This can be overcome, and children's motivation sustained, by opportunities to join with peers from other schools, for special project work, workshops or seminars and other extra-curricular activities. Teachers can benefit from working with teachers in other schools to produce extension and enrichment materials and to discuss successful strategies they use in managing activities.

Links with schools in the next phase

Help can sometimes be sought from the school in the next phase to which the children will transfer. Teachers in the next phase will have more subject-specific expertise and be able to advise on suitable programmes of study, materials and resources. In some instances schools can make arrangements for staff from the next phase to provide some teaching for certain groups of children or to demonstrate approaches to teaching higher levels of learning in a subject. Other examples of flexible practice include secondary schools providing weekly sessions for children drawn from the feeder schools, where subject topics can be explored beyond the level that is followed in the primary school. There can be many other such imaginative and creative ways of collaborating and pooling resources in order to meet children's needs.

Links with colleges and institutes of higher education

Some young people with exceptional ability or talent in a specific aspect of their learning may outgrow the resources of their school before they reach the age of 16 or 18. 'Fast-tracking' and early entry to public examinations may not solve the problem. In fact, such courses of action are likely to result in schools needing to provide alternative or additional courses of study to 'fill the gap' once the examinations have been taken. The new National Curriculum Orders have validated schools' ability to be flexible and adapt the curriculum to suit the needs of students. The potential in local colleges and universities has not been fully explored by most schools. Links between college departments and schools and between college students and pupils have often been found to bring considerable benefit in opening up the range of expertise and support available.

Local business and industry

One of the priorities of the Excellence in Cities initiative is the development and the fostering of links with business and industry. The potential for supporting the educational experiences of more able pupils and those with exceptional talents is enormous. The use of business people as mentors, work-experience placements in less familiar and challenging environments, seminars and workshops held in and out of school, the sponsoring of research projects and residencies with local artists and performers all offer opportunities to broaden the horizons of young people and keep them excited about their learning.

CHAPTER 13

Looking to the future

Developments in education

In 1985, when the first edition of this book was published, provision for able pupils in UK schools was patchy, to say the least. Despite many individual examples of good practice and some interesting initiatives in a number of Local Authorities, there was no national drive to help schools extend the curriculum. The education of able pupils was not a major priority for most schools. Her Majesty's Inspectorate (HMI) reported on several occasions that many able pupils were not receiving the attention they deserved and were not achieving as well as they might (HMI 1979, 1985, 1992). The challenges that can face very able children were not fully appreciated. The emphasis of the first edition was therefore to identify the issues and to press the case for better understanding and provision.

The educational world looks very different now from that of the 1980s. The many changes that have taken place in every aspect of education have 'altered the landscape' of provision in schools. Most recently, in the last two years, the education of able pupils has been given a national prominence. Schools and teachers are becoming increasingly aware of the shortcomings that exist and of the work that needs to be done to ensure that all pupils receive an education that meets their needs. The case for able pupils no longer has to be made. But developments are still needed. Schools will have to continue to respond and adapt to the changes that are taking place in society.

The most significant changes likely to take place in education during the next few years will be in the use of information technology and the development of interactive, computer-based learning. This is already bringing about fundamental changes in the way schools operate. In the future, boundaries between education and training, classrooms and work environments will become less clear, and divisions between different phases of education will become increasingly blurred (Wood 1993). We have already seen such changes taking place with developments in the 14–19 curriculum and the introduction of courses and qualifications such as GNVQ and NVQ which cross the secondary/tertiary divide. The globalisation of knowledge through developments in the internet is revolutionising the way children and young people gain access to information and pursue their studies.

The future could look much brighter for children with exceptional ability. The freeing up of classrooms from the traditionally organised, teacher-dependent form of working to one where students can be released to pursue their enquiries and tailor their pace of learning through the use of modern technology may well resolve some of the current tensions. The decreased reliance on books, pens and paper as a consequence of laptop computing, communications technology and large-scale multi-base databases may well eliminate the source of much of the frustration that has limited the progress and achievement of many young people in the past. Teachers are likely to spend less time imparting information and testing its reception, and more on providing frameworks for project work and on attending to individual pupils' learning process and progress.

The revolution in communications technology from using computers to access information on an individual basis to using the technology for group-based work and networking, is already under way. There is evidence from the USA that this is the future for education and similar trends are detectable in Britain.

Interest is also being generated by recent research into the process of learning and the need to take into account the multi-dimensional nature of different human abilities. In the past, there has been too little regard for different learning styles or the importance of using all the different modalities to reinforce understanding and skills (Smith 1998). Brain-based learning addresses this by taking account of the relative functions of the different hemispheres in the brain and how connections are made. Based on the evidence of how learning is made most effective, this approach to learning aims to provide experiences that combine visual, auditory and kinaesthetic approaches to reinforce the development of new skills and understanding and embed the new learning. As its success also depends on fostering self-esteem and the reduction of stress, as well as providing a high level of challenge, it should benefit children with exceptional abilities as well as their peers. Children should thereby be better able to demonstrate their potential for making connections and linking ideas, as well as fostering their imagination and talents. More creative and unusual patterns of thinking and learning would also be legitimised.

If this is the future, the impact on how young people with exceptional ability are perceived, and how they therefore develop through infancy to adulthood, will be profound. The isolation that has damaged the childhood and adolescence of many young people whose intellectual development and academic interests are out of line from their peer group could be avoided. With different patterns of study being the norm, and the learning environment extending beyond the boundaries of the school and the classroom, young people will be free to establish friendships and working relationships that are not restricted by a class group or age-related groupings. With less anxiety and concern about *how* their learning needs are to be handled, parents and teachers will have more time and energy to concentrate on the building of relationships and on fostering those opportunities and links that underpin the quality of our lives together.

Creating a climate for growth

The educational scene in Britain has been revolutionised during the past 20 years. What has not changed is the human dimension to bringing up children, be it in the role of parent or in the role of teacher. Growing up is a fascinating process, full of excitements and possibilities. Living and working with children who have exceptional abilities is a privilege. But it has its challenges!

It is challenging for the children themselves because they have to learn to accept themselves as they are, to live with the differences they perceive between themselves and others, to have the courage to be creative and to take risks. In order to be accepted and valued by others it is equally important that they learn to accept and value those with whom they live and share within the community, and that they remain optimistic and positive about their relationships.

It is challenging for parents. They have to provide an environment in which the children feel secure, where the rights of all family members are respected and the needs and demands of one do not override the concern for others. While parents have to ensure that the interests and abilities of an exceptional child are adequately supported, they must also take care that their own hopes and aspirations, as parents, do not become a burden for their child.

It is challenging for teachers and schools. They have to recognise that all children, including the most able, have a right to experiences that enable them to progress, to work at their own pace and to have their talents and abilities properly taken into account.

And finally, it is challenging for all of us to manage our relationships and our response to one another in ways that are constructive and encourage trust. To ensure that children grow up healthily we need to create the kind of nurturing environments that help children, like plants, develop sturdy roots that support and sustain their unique development.

In nurturing homes children know they are loved for themselves with all their gifts, their faults, their talents and their idiosyncrasies. They learn they are important because people love them for themselves and not for how they look or what they do. They find that they can try things out and test themselves in safety, because it is all right to make mistakes and fail. They are taught they are special, because every human being is special, and not because they learn faster or slower than others, or do clever and surprising things. They learn they can expect to be treated fairly and with respect, and that they in turn have a responsibility towards others.

Nurturing classrooms and schools are environments in which children can be themselves, without embarrassment or fear, where they can display their talents naturally through all the activities they undertake. In nurturing classrooms children can ask challenging questions without fear of mockery, learning is presented as exciting, and effort and achievement of all kinds are celebrated and rewarded. Nurturing schools organise activities that allow all children to learn with and from each other, provide opportunities in school to compensate for what is not available in pupils' homes, keep a watchful eye on the climate in every classroom, and make clear the message that we achieve more together than on our own.

Behavioural checklists to help in the recognition of exceptional ability

Checklists, such as the one given here, are not tests to determine whether or not a particular child is exceptionally able. Each child is unique, and any one child may or may not show some, all or none of the characteristics described. But checklists can prove helpful in alerting parents and teachers to the possibility that they may be misjudging some of their children, and in encouraging them to look for positive signs of talents that they may have so far failed to acknowledge.

Many different checklists have been put forward, some fairly short and concise, others of great length and all-embracing detail. The one given below attempts to include the most commonly mentioned features, without becoming unnecessarily complex.

Exceptionally able children may demonstrate some of the following:

- Great intellectual curiosity: A desire to know the whys and the hows of all events; provocative and searching questions; dissatisfaction with simple explanations
- Superior reasoning ability: Ability to deal with abstract concepts, to generalise from specific facts, to see connections between events
- Unusual persistence: A determination to complete tasks to their own satisfaction; ability to concentrate for long periods of time
- Exceptional speed of thought, rapid response to new ideas
- Ability to learn quickly and easily: Understanding a task often before the full instructions or explanations have been given; needing little or no practice to acquire competence
- Good memory: Apparent lack of need to rehearse learning or to revise
- Extensive vocabulary: Heightened sensitivity to language generally; insistence on the precise meaning of words; delight in technical terms
- Acute powers of observation: Close attention to detail
- Vivid imagination, both verbally and in other creative work such as drawing and model-making
- Divergent thinking: tendency to look for unusual ways of solving problems

- Great initiative: Preference for independent work
- Highly developed sense of humour, often esoteric; delight in verbal puns
- Unusually high personal standards: Frustration if they cannot achieve the excellence they demand of themselves; perfectionist approach, not satisfied with approval from others
- Impatience, both with self and with others: Intolerance towards others less able than themselves; contempt for adults who talk down to them
- Sensitivity and highly strung behaviour: Quick to react to disapproval; easily frustrated; highly perceptive
- Wide range of interests: Hobbies that are sometimes unusual and which are followed with great enthusiasm and competence; often keen collectors
- Extensive knowledge and expertise in a particular subject
- Preference for the company of older children and adults: Boredom with the company and interests of peers
- Desire to direct others in play and in group activities
- Preoccupation with matters of philosophical and universal concern, such as the nature of man, the meaning of life, the concept of space, etc.

However, exceptionally able children may not necessarily show their talents in obvious or acceptable ways. They may for instance be:

- unusually articulate, but unable to produce good or neatly written work
- restless, inattentive, given to daydreaming
- keen to get attention by playing the role of class clown
- reticent, or reluctant to demonstrate their knowledge or ability
- unwilling to follow instructions for class tasks, preferring to do things their own way
- unenthusiastic about classwork in general: may appear ungracious, uncooperative or apathetic
- hypercritical, persistently questioning the reasons given
- quick to note inconsistencies, to point out errors of logic or information
- uncomfortably forthright in their assessment of situations and in their ability to recognise discrepancies between what people think and what they do
- withdrawn; reluctant to take part in group tasks; appearing to prefer their own company.

None of these behaviours is proof of high ability, but they can alert adults to the need to question why the child is behaving in that way.

References

Ballinger, M., Gardner, R. and Blagg, N. (1988) *Somerset Thinking Skills Course*. Oxford: Blackwell.

Bloom, B. S. (1956) *Taxonomy of Education Objectives*. London: Methuen.

Bloom, B. S. (1985) *Developing Talent in Young People*. New York: Ballantine Books.

De Bono, E. (1970) *Lateral Thinking*. London: Penguin.

Deaux, K. and Emswiller, T. (1974) 'Explanations of successful performances on sex-linked tasks', *Journal of Personality and Social Psychology* **2**, 80–5.

DES (1989) *Standards in Education 1988–89): The Annual Report of HM Senior Chief Inspector of Schools*. London: HMSO.

DfEE (1994) *Code of Practice on the Identification and Assessment of Special Educational Needs*. London: HMSO.

DfEE (1999) *Excellence in Cities*. London: DfEE Publications.

DfEE (2000) *National Literacy and Numeracy Strategies: Guidance on teaching able children*. London: DfEE Publications.

DfEE and QCA (1999) *The National Curriculum: Handbook*. London: DfEE.

Eyre, D. (1997) *Able Children in Ordinary Schools*. London: David Fulton Publishers.

Eyre, D. and Fuller, M. (1993) *Year 6 Teachers and More Able Pupils*. Oxford: National Primary Centre, Oxfordshire County Council.

Feuerstein, R. (1980) *Instrumental Enrichment*. Maryland: University of Baltimore Park Press.

Fisher, R. (1995) *Teaching Children to Think*. Cheltenham: Stanley Thornes Publishers.

Fox, L. H. and Zimmerman, W. (1985) 'Gifted women', in Freeman, J. (ed.) *The Psychology of Gifted Children: Perspectives on development and education*. Chichester: Wiley.

Freeman, J. (1991a) *Bright as a Button*. London: Optima.

Freeman, J. (1991b) *Gifted Children Growing Up*. London: Cassell.

Freeman, J. (1995) *How to Raise a Bright Child: Practical ways to encourage your child's talent from 0–5 years*. London: Vermilion.

Freeman, J. (1996) *Clever Children: Handbook for parents.* London: Hamlyn Books.

Freeman, J. (2001) *Gifted Children Grown Up.* London: David Fulton Publishers.

Freeman, J., Span, P. and Wagner, H. (1995) *Actualizing Talent: A lifelong challenge.* London: Cassell.

Gardner, H. (1983) *Frames of Mind: The theory of multiple intelligences.* New York: Basic Books.

Gardner, H, (1990) *Frames of Mind: The theory of multiple intelligences,* 2nd edn. New York: Basic Books.

George, D. (1997) *The Challenge of the Able Child.* London: David Fulton Publishers.

Gomme, S. (2000) Chapter 4, 'The role of the family', in Stopper, M. J. (ed.) *Meeting the Social and Emotional Need of Gifted and Talented Children.* London: David Fulton Publishers.

Gottfried, A. *et al.* (1994) *Gifted IQ: Early developmental aspects. The Fullerton Longitudinal Study.* New York: Plenum Press.

Heatherington, L. *et al.* (1989) 'Towards an understanding of the social consequences of feminine immodesty about personal achievement', *Sex Roles* **20**, 371–80.

HMI (1979) *Aspects of Secondary Education.* London: HMSO.

HMI (1985) *Education Observed 3: Good Teachers.* London: HMSO.

HMI (1992) *Provision for Highly Able Pupils in Maintained Schools.* London: HMSO.

House of Commons Select Committee report (1999) *Highly Able Children.* London: HMSO.

Howe, M. J. A. (1996) Presentation to the British Psychological Society Annual Meeting, March 1996. Quoted in the *Observer*, 14 April.

Hymer, B. and Harbron, N. (1998) *Early Transfer: A good move?* NACE journal Spring 1998, 38–47.

Kellmer Pringle, M. (1970) *Able Misfits: A study of educational and behavioural difficulties of 103 very intelligent children.* London: Longman/National Children's Bureau.

Kelly, G. (1971) Chapter 1, 'The psychology of personal constructs', in Bannister, D. and Fransella, F. (eds) *Inquiring Man: The theory of personal constructs,* 11–43. London: Penguin.

Kolb, D. A. and Fry, R. (1975) Towards an applied theory of experiential learning, in Cooper, C. L. (ed.) *Theories of Group Processes,* 33–58. London: John Wiley.

Lake, M. (1990) *Primary Thinking Skills Project.* Birmingham: Questions Publishing Company.

Lee-Corbin, H. and Denicolo, P. (1998) *Recognising and Supporting Able Children in Primary Schools.* London: David Fulton Publishers.

Leyden, S. (1995) 'Why Not Talk to the Pupils'. *Flying High* (journal of the National Association for Able Children in Education), spring 1995, issue 2.

Lipman, M. (1991) *Thinking in Education.* Cambridge: Cambridge University Press.

Maslow, A. H. (1954) *Motivation and Personality.* New York: Harper.

Montgomery, D. (1996) *Educating the Able.* London: Cassell.

Murray, L. (1997) Post-natal depression research findings. Quoted in *The Observer*, October.

Murris, K. (1992) *Teaching Philosophy with Picture Books.* London: Infonet Publications.

Norwich, B. (1996) 'Special needs education or education for all: connective specialism and ideological impurity', *British Journal of Special Education* **23** (3), 100–4.

Nottinghamshire County Council (1999) *Providing for Able Pupils and Those with Exceptional Talent:* manual of guidance for schools. Nottinghamshire County Council.

O'Brien, P. (1998a) *Teaching Scientifically Able Pupils in the Primary School.* Oxford: NACE.

O'Brien, P. (1998b) *Teaching Scientifically Able Pupils in the Secondary School.* Oxford: NACE.

OfSTED (1998) *Handbook for Inspecting Schools (Secondary, Primary and Special).* London: HMSO.

OfSTED (2000) *Evaluating Educational Inclusion.* London: OfSTED.

Osborne, E. (1994) Some implications of the theoretical framework, in Dowling, E. and Osborne, E. (eds) *The Family and the School: A joint systems approach to problems with children*, 31–3. London: Routledge.

Qualifications and Curriculum Authority (QCA) (2001) *Guidance on Teaching Gifted and Talented Pupils.* DfES Publications and on www.nc.uk.net/gt/general. London: QCA.

Resnick, L. B. (1989) *Knowing, Learning and Instruction: Essays in honour of Robert Glaser.* Hillsdale: New York.

Schools Curriculum and Assessment Authority (SCAA) (1997) *Making Effective Use of Key Stage 2 Assessments.* Hayes: SCAA Publications.

Smith, A. (1998) *Accelerated Learning in the Classroom.* Stafford: Network Educational Press.

Sternberg, R. J. (1985) *Beyond IQ: A triarchic theory of human intelligence.* New York: Cambridge University Press.

Storr, A. (1988) *The School of Genius.* London: Andre Deutsch.

Teare, B. (1997) *Effective Provision for Able and Talented Children.* Stafford: Network Educational Press.

Thomas, L. and Harri-Augstein, S. (1985) *Self-Organised Learning: Foundations of a conversational science for psychology.* London: Routledge and Kegan Paul.

Vail, P. (1979) *The World of the Gifted Child*. New York: Walker.

Walden, R. and Walkerdine, V. (1985) 'Girls and mathematics: from primary to secondary schooling', *Bedford Way Papers* **24**, London: Institute of Education, University of London.

Wall, W. D. (1968) *Adolescents in School and Society*. Slough: NFER.

Wallace, B. (2000) *Teaching the Very Able Child*. London: David Fulton Publishers.

Wood, D. (1988) *How Children Think and Learn*. Oxford: Blackwell.

Wood, D. (1993) 'The Classroom of 2015', *National Commission on Education: Briefing Paper 20*. London: Paul Hamlyn.

Wood, D. (1999) *How Children Think and Learn*. Oxford: Blackwell.

Further reading

Clarke, C. and Callow, R. (1998) *Educating Able Children: Resource issues and processes for teachers*. London: David Fulton Publishers.

Eyre, D. and Marjoram, T. (1990) *Enriching and Extending the National Curriculum*. London: Kegan Paul.

Freeman, J. (1979) *Gifted Children: Their identification and development in a social context*. Lancaster: MTP Press.

Freeman, J. (1994) 'Some emotional aspects of being gifted', *Journal of the Education of the Gifted*, **17**, 180–97.

Fryer, M. (1996) *Creative Teaching and Learning*. London: Chapman.

Howe, M. J. A. (1990) *The Origins of Exceptional Abilities*. Oxford: Blackwell.

Lipman, M. (1991) *Thinking of Education*. Cambridge: Cambridge University Press.

Montgomery, D. (1996) *Educating the Able*. London: Cassell.

Quinn, V. (1997) *Critical Thinking in Young Minds*. London: David Fulton Publishers.

Robinson, K. (ed.) (1990) *The Arts 5-16: A curriculum framework*. Essex: Oliver Boyd.

Stopper, M. J. (ed.) (2000) *Meeting the Social and Emotional Needs of Gifted and Talented Children*. NACE/David Fulton Publishers.

Vernon, P. E., Adamson, G. and Vernon, D. (1977) *The Psychology and Education of Gifted Children*. London: Methuen.

Wallace, B. (2000) *Teaching the Very Able Child: Developing a policy and adopting strategies for provision*. NACE/David Fulton Publishers.

Publications which provide practical guidance for structuring and planning the curriculum

Bloom, B. S. (1956) *Taxonomy of Education Objectives*. London: Methuen.

De Bono, E. (1976) *Teaching Thinking*. London: Temple-Smith.

Dean, G. (1998) *Challenging the More Able Language User*. NACE/David Fulton Publishers.

Evans, L. and Goodhew, G. (1997) *Providing for Able Children*. Dunstable: Folens Press.

Eyre, D. (1997) *Able Children in Ordinary Schools*. London: David Fulton Publishers.

Eyre, D. and Marjoram, T. (1990) *Enriching and Extending the National Curriculum*. London: Kegan Paul.

Fisher, R. (1987) *Problem Solving in Primary Schools*. Cheltenham: Stanley Thornes Publishers.

Fisher, R. (1995) *Teaching Children to Think*. Cheltenham: Stanley Thornes Publishers.

Fowler, W. F. (1990) *Talking from Infancy: How to nurture and cultivate Early Language Development*. Cambridge, MA: Brookline Books.

George, D. (1995) *Gifted Education: Identification and provision*. London: David Fulton Publishers.

Kennard, R. (2001) *Teaching Mathematically Able Children*. London: David Fulton Publishers.

Kerry, T. (1981) *Teaching Bright Children*. London: Macmillan.

Kerry, T. (1982) *Effective Questioning*. London: Macmillan.

Koshy, V. (2000) *Teaching Mathematics to Able Children*. London: David Fulton Publishers.

Nottinghamshire County Council (1999) *Able Pupils: Providing for Able Pupils and Those with Exceptional Talent*. Nottinghamshire Education Department.

O'Brien, P. (1998a) *Teaching Scientifically Able Pupils in the Primary School*. Oxford: NACE Publications.

O'Brien, P. (1998b) *Teaching Scientifically Able Pupils in the Secondary School*. Oxford: NACE Publications.

Qualifications and Curriculum Authority (QCA) (2001) *Guidance on Teaching Gifted and Talented Pupils*. DfES Publications and on www.nc.uk.net/gt/general

Renzulli, J. S. (1977) *The Enrichment Triad Model: A guide for developing defensible programs for the gifted and talented*. Wethersfield, CT: Creative Learning Press.

Smith, A. (1996) *Accelerated Learning in the Classroom*. Stafford: Network Educational Press.

Smith, A. (1998) *Accelerated Learning in Practice*. Stafford: Network Educational Press Ltd.

Teare, B. (1996) *A School Policy on Provision for Able and Talented Pupils*. Oxford: NACE Publications.

Teare, B. (1997) *Effective Provision for Able and Talented Children*. Stafford. Network Education Press.

Teare, B. (1999) *Effective Resources for Able and Talented Children*. Stafford: Network Educational Press.

Wallace, B. (ed.) (2001) *Teaching Thinking Skills Across the Curriculum*. NACE/ David Fulton Publishers.

Willings, D. (1980) *The Creatively Gifted: Recognising and developing the creative personality*. Cambridge: Woodhead-Faulkner.

Wragg, E. R. (1993) *Questioning*. London: Routledge.

Useful sources of ideas and materials for activities at home and school

Bowkett, S. (1997) *Imagine That… A handbook for creative learning activities in the classroom*. Trowbridge. Redwood Books.

Casey, R. and Koshy, V. (1995) *Bright Challenge*. Cheltenham: Stanley Thornes. Publishers. (Materials for 7- to 12-year-olds.)

De Bono, E. (1970) *Lateral Thinking*. London: Penguin.

De Bono, E. (1973) *Cort Thinking*. Direct Educational Services, 35 Albert Street., Blandford, Dorset, DT11 7HZ.

De Bono, E. (1975) *Think Links*. Direct Educational Services, 35 Albert Street., Blandford, Dorset, DT11 7HZ.

De Bono, E. (1992) *Teach Your Child How to Think*. Harmondsworth: Penguin. (A book for parents to encourage creative/lateral thinking.)

Dickinson, C. (1996) *Effective Learning Activities*. Stafford: Network Educational Press. (Second title in a series of handbooks which provide practical ideas for raising pupil achievement. It shows how teachers can plan activities that challenge able children as well as support the less able within the current curriculum structures.)

Evans, L. and Goodhew, G. (1997) *Providing for Able Pupils*. Dunstable: Folens Press.

Fisher, R. Occasional Papers: including *Teaching Thinking; Creative Thinking; Questioning for Thinking; Moral Education; The Thinking Child; Stories for Thinking*. The Centre for Thinking Skills, West London Institute, 300 St Margaret's Road, Twickenham, London, SW1 1BT. (A series of booklets with both theoretical discussion and practical examples for activities to promote effective thinking strategies.)

Fisher, R. (1994) *Active Art*. Cheltenham: Stanley Thornes Publishers.

Fisher, R. (1996) *Stories for Thinking*. (1997) *Games for Thinking*. (1998) *Maths for Thinking*. Oxford: Nash Pollock Publishing. (A very useful set of books providing a wealth of ideas for developing and extending primary pupils' thinking skills.)

Freeman, J. (1995) *How to Raise a Bright Child: Practical ways to encourage your child's talents from 0–5 years*. London: Vermilion.

Freeman, J. (1996) *Clever Children: A handbook for parents*. London: Hamlyn.

Gardiner, A. (1987) *Mathematical Puzzling*. Oxford: Oxford University Press.

Gardiner, A. (1996) *Mathematical Challenges*. Cambridge: Cambridge University Press.

Jackson, B. (1980) *Your Exceptional Child*. London: Fontana.

Lake, M. (1991) *Brill the Brave*. Birmingham: Questions Publishing. (Stories used as the basis for philosophical enquiry in the Primary Thinking Skills Project.)

Murchinson, J. (1996) *Maths Problems for Gifted and Talented Students*. Colchester: Phoenix Education, Claire Publications and Jonathan Press.

Other Contacts, organisations and further information

Association of Teachers of Mathematics Publications
7 Shaftesbury Street, Derby, DE23 8YB

BAAS (British Association for the Advancement of Science)
23 Saville Row, London, EC1A 9DD

Centre for Philosophy for Children
K. Morris, Old Acres, Charvil, Berks, RG10 9QL

Centre for Thinking Skills
Brunel University, 300 St Margaret's Road, Twickenham, TW1 1PT

Children of High Intelligence (CHI)
Box 4222, London, SE22 8XG

Mathematics Association
259 London Road, Leicester, LE2 2BE

National Association for Able Children in Education (NACE)
PO Box 242, Arnold's Way, Oxford, OX2 9FR
e-mail: info@nace.co.uk

National Association for Gifted Children (NAGC)
Suite 14, Challenge House, Sherwood Drive, Bletchley, Milton Keynes, MK3 6DP
e-mail: amazingchildren@nagcbritain.org.uk

National Mentoring Network
First Floor, Charles House, Albert Street, Eccles, Manchester, M30 0PD

NRICH
University of Cambridge, School of Education, 17 Trumpington Street, Cambridge, CB2 1QA
www.nrich.math.org.uk/ablepupils

UK Mathematics Trust
Maths Challenges Office, School of Mathematics, University of Leeds, LS2 9JT

Local Authorities
Educational Psychology Services: Educational psychologists working within Local Education Authorities may be able to offer advice, counselling and support to both children and their families as well as working with schools on developing their provision for individual needs. Parents can usually make contact either directly or through their child's school.

Other Services
Schools can advise parents on the facilities within the community for children with interests in the performing arts or sport.

Local libraries and arts centres are invaluable sources of materials, activities and advice.

Index

Lightning Source UK Ltd.
Milton Keynes UK
UKOW06f1919271013

219890UK00008B/109/P